HOW TO
SELL MORE

The Daily Express Guides

The Daily Express and Kogan Page have joined forces to publish a series of practical guides offering no-nonsense advice on a wide range of financial, legal and business topics.

Whether you want to manage your money better, make more money, get a new business idea off the ground – and make sure its legal – there's a Daily Express Guide for you.

Titles published so far are:

Great Ideas for Making Money
Niki Chesworth

Your Money
How to Make the Most of it
Niki Chesworth

You and the Law
A Simple Guide to All Your Legal Problems
Susan Singleton

How to Cut Your Tax Bill Without Breaking the Law
Grant Thornton, Chartered Accountants

Be Your Own Boss!
How to Set Up a Successful Small Business
David Mc Mullan

Readymade Business Letters That Get Results
Jim Douglas

Available from all good bookshops, or to obtain further information please contact the publishers at the address below:

Kogan Page Ltd
120 Pentonville Rd
London N1 9JN
Tel: 071-278 0433
Fax: 071-837 6348

Daily Express

HOW TO SELL MORE

A Guide for Small Business

N E I L J O H N S O N

KOGAN
PAGE

To Mark, Karina and the Baby, with fondest love

The right of Neil Johnson to be identified as author of this work has been asserted by him in accordance with the Copyright, Designs and Patents Act 1988.

First published in 1994.

Kogan Page Limited
120 Pentonville Road
London N1 9JN

© Neil Johnson 1994

British Library Cataloguing in Publication Data
A CIP record for this book is available from the British Library.

ISBN 0-7494-1333-6

Typeset by Saxon Graphics Ltd, Derby
Printed and bound in Great Britain by Clays Ltd, St Ives plc

Contents

What this book is all about

This is a no-nonsense sales book for business people

- If you run a small business (with fewer than ten employees) and want to improve your sales as quickly and efficiently as possible, this is the book for you!
- It contains everything you need to know to master the art of selling and then apply it to your business.
- It is packed with simple, practical examples to help you start selling *today!*
- If you read it carefully and practise its recommendations, you will never look back!

This book will work for you

The ideas in this book are very simple but very effective. By following them, I managed to raise the monthly sales of a small business from £5000 to over £100,000.

What you will learn by reading this book

- *How to sell almost anything to anyone*
  By following the Classic Sales Method – an all-purpose sales method, used by many of the world's top salespeople.
- *How to increase the sales of your business*
  By following six simple steps to sales success:

  1. How to organise yourself (page 31).
  2. How to inject real sales power into your routines (page 43).
  3. How to sell more to your present customers (page 57).
  4. How to find new customers (page 71).
  5. How to master the technique of telephone selling (page 81).
  6. How to learn the art of face-to-face selling (page 97).

The terms used in this book

To make this book as readable as possible, I have chosen to avoid writing he/she, him/her, his/her whenever gender is mentioned. Instead, I use a single masculine gender. I emphasise that this is done purely for stylistic reasons and that, therefore, the words he, him and his are at all times interchangeable with the words she, her and hers. For similar stylistic reasons, the word 'product' is nearly always interchangeable with the word 'service', and the word 'customer' with the word 'buyer'.

Neil Johnson, 1994

1
The Classic Sales Method

As long as unpredictable creatures called human beings do the buying, selling will never be an exact science and no sales method will ever be foolproof. Indeed, it is probably true to say that no salesperson will ever succeed in selling to more than a fraction of his contacts.

Nevertheless, nearly all buying and selling is governed by a number of key principles that must be understood and applied by any aspiring salesperson.

The Classic Sales Method is a synthesis of the most important of these elementary principles. Whatever type of business you are in, your best chance of increasing your sales is to learn and master this method.

The four steps of the Classic Sales Method

1. Find out the needs of your buyer.
2. Satisfy those needs.
3. Answer any objections.
4. Push for the order.

Find out the needs of your buyer

This is the first step that any salesperson should take when dealing with a buyer. If you can do this successfully, you have every chance of making a sale. If not, your chances of selling anything are slim.

Why are needs important? What are they?

Needs are important because, according to the experts, they are the reason we buy things: we buy in order to satisfy our needs.

In this context, the word 'needs' refers to a buyer's particular way of looking at things. It includes his personal concerns or personal priorities as well as his more obvious needs. To demonstrate the point, we shall divide all buyers into two groups: individual buyers (buying for themselves) and commercial buyers (buying on behalf of companies).

Individual buyers

Examples of different needs:

- *Janet*, a housewife, walks into a shop and buys a £65 kettle. It is intended as a wedding present for a relative.

  Her need? She feels that she needs to show off her generosity and wealth.
- *John*, a businessman dining in a restaurant, orders a £200 bottle of wine. He does this because he is entertaining an important business client.

  His need? He feels he must impress and indulge his guest in order to clinch the sale.
- *Bridgette*, a single, 24-year-old, books herself a whole Saturday of beauty treatments.

  Her need? She feels that she needs to improve her appearance in order to dazzle her evening date.
- *Terry* and *June*, a married couple who belong to the local 'smart set', buy a new fitted kitchen for the second time in two years.

  Their need? They feel that they need to maintain their social standing and influence.

Points

- Notice how 'individual' the above needs are. The fact is, most people have their own unique attitudes to what is worth buying.
- As I hope you can see from the above examples, you should never confuse the *need* of a particular buyer with *what is good for him*.

Commercial buyers

You may think that these buyers have less opportunity to indulge their individual preferences; in reality they have considerable leeway.

Examples of different needs:

- *Arthur* is the headmaster of a secondary school, whose sixth-form computer class needs a replacement computer.

  Arthur's need? He feels that he needs to buy a computer that is both reliable and durable and comes with efficient after-sales service.

- *Bill* is the maintenance manager of a large insurance company, responsible for all maintenance work at the company's head office. He is looking for a firm of contractors to handle day-to-day electrical repairs.

  Bill's need? He feels that it would be best to appoint a small, responsible contractor capable of a flexible response to problems.

- *Chris* owns a small but thriving distribution company in north London. In one of his periodic fits of cost-cutting, he rings up a number of computer stationery suppliers to try to negotiate an extra discount in return for an exclusive contract to supply.

  Chris's need? He is looking for the cheapest deal and is uninterested in issues like speed of service, product range or payment terms, even though all these matters can affect the final cost.

- *Dave* is the bathroom-materials buyer for a large chain of DIY stores.

  Dave's need? He feels that his main need is to buy tiles that sell. He therefore prefers to buy bland and inoffensive designs with the widest popular appeal.

- *Edward* is the thrifty MD of a medium-sized publishing company. To him, money spent on new office furniture is money wasted. It never occurs to him that by replacing the old, rather threadbare, furniture in the company's reception area and boardroom, he might impress his customers and enhance his business.

  Edward's need? He feels he has no need.

Points

- Notice that, despite having a tangible buying need, each of the above buyers has his own particular attitude to what and how he buys. This is another way of saying that each of them has his own particular need.
- As in our earlier set of examples, notice that a buyer's need is never either obvious or necessarily good for him.

  For example, *Arthur* may be better advised to buy several cheaper computers (and properly supervise their use) rather than one durable model; equally, *Bill* may do better by appointing a larger, reliable firm of contractors (and impress the need for flexibility upon them), and *Chris* may do better by striking a deal with a firm capable of supplying *all* his stationery/office equipment requirements, rather than just computer stationery.

As for *Dave*, he may be better advised to widen his range of tiles thus avoiding the risk of customers going elsewhere for more interesting designs, and *Edward* to start rethinking his company's image.

The importance of knowing a buyer's particular needs

Since the experts say that we buy in order to satisfy our needs, it follows that, if you can discover the needs of your buyer, your chances of offering him something he wants are vastly improved. Thus, we arrive at the fundamental starting point of every sale.

As a salesperson, your first task is to find out the particular needs of your buyer. Only when you know these, can you begin to sell.

How do you find out a buyer's needs?

The short answer to this is, *ask*. The only person who can tell you a particular buyer's needs is the buyer himself.

Three tips on how to ask buyers about their needs

First, and most important of all, do not be in the least bit coy about asking lots of questions. The more you ask, the more you will find out. No salesperson ever lost a sale because he knew too much about his customer!

Second, unless you have a photographic memory, do yourself a favour and get into the habit of using a *checklist* to remind you of what questions to ask - espically if you deal with telephone enquiries. By having your next question already jotted down in front of you, you can concentrate on listening to the buyer's replies as well as perfecting your delivery.

Third, if at all possible, avoid mentioning price until the end. Despite what you may think, price is rarely the most important consideration for most buyers. Instead, they are usually much more concerned about quality, convenience and reliability.

Example

You are a hotel owner. It is 1 September and the secretary to the MD of a local company rings for details concerning Christmas parties. Following the Classic Sales Method, you avoid talking about what your hotel offers until you have discovered the particular needs of your customer.

You: Before I go into detail about things, let me just ask you a couple of quick questions. For example, what date do you want to have your party?

Sec: 14 December.

You: What is the minimum number of guests likely to be?

Sec: Between 40 and 45.

You: What sort of meal did you have in mind: buffet or sit-down?

Sec: Sit-down, depending on price of course. How much do you charge?

You: I'll come to that in a moment. What about any special menus: are there any vegetarians among you?

Sec: Actually, now that you mention it, our finance director is a vegetarian. Something to do with his heart, I think.

Sec: Fine. One of my chefs is a vegetarian so we can fix up something nice, no problem. What about drinks with the meal: do you want wine?

Sec: Oh yes. Definitely.

You: What about the directors: are any of them wine buffs?

Sec: One or two maybe.

You: OK, you can tell them that we have some really excellent vintages. Now what about music: are you interested in having a live band or a disco, or what?

Sec: We'd like a disco. Would that be extra?

You: Hold on, I'll give you all the prices in a tick. What about transport: do you want taxis ordered, or do you want to do all that yourself?

Sec: Oh, I hadn't thought of that.

You: I just thought I'd mention it because we have an arrangement with a local firm and, let's face it, taxis can be rather few and far between over Christmas.

Sec: You're quite right. I'll check on that.

You: What about rooms: is anyone likely to be staying overnight?

Sec: Yes. I'm not sure how many exactly – at least three or four, maybe more.

You: OK, now what sort of budget are you working to? What's your top figure, just to give me some idea?

Sec: I can go up to about £20–£22 per person, but only if it's worth it.

You: Right. Let me check on a couple of things and I'll fax you all the details first thing tomorrow. How's that?

Points

- Notice how you gradually build up a picture of what the buyer needs or might need, and what commercial potential there is in the deal.
- Notice how you discover a few small but useful details. For instance, one director is a vegetarian, one or two directors are wine buffs, three or four people will need rooms overnight.
- Notice also how you avoid any mention of how much you charge (you intend to work out what price to charge later) and how you make a point of asking what the company's maximum budget is. OK, you may not always be told but there is no harm in asking: it is vital information after all.
- Notice, finally, how you manage to slip a few sales points into your questioning. For example, your vegetarian chef, your vintage wines and your arrangement with the taxi firm. Although your listener may not have been a decision-maker, these little sales points will definitely help to form an impression in her mind, and they will almost certainly be passed on to the decision-makers themselves.

Never try to sell to someone before you know his needs

The biggest mistake a salesperson can make is to start trying to sell to a customer before knowing what that customer wants/needs. However confident you are – that you know what a customer wants – never let this stop you from double-checking: ask the customer himself and make certain.

Examples

One evening, *Barry*, a plumber, visits a house to quote for the job of installing a central-heating system. After being shown over the house by the owner and making a note of the relevant dimensions, together with the number, type and locations of radiators required, he quickly assesses the amount of work involved and gives the houseowner an approximate quote. He is then asked when he could do the job and replies that he can start in about ten days. The owner then thanks him and says goodbye. Barry never hears from him again. Where does Barry go wrong?

Barry's mistake
His basic mistake is to treat the whole process as a mathematical rather than a selling exercise. Giving a quote to someone is always a selling exercise and, as you should now know, in any sales situation, the first thing that any salesperson should do is *find out the buyer's needs*. This is what Barry fails to do.

Barry assumes too much
For instance, he falls straight into the trap of assuming that the owner wants a heating system installed in order to heat the house. In fact, the owner may have no real interest in the warmth of the house. He may not actually live there and he may intend to sell it as soon as possible. He may want to have a central-heating system installed purely in order to boost the sale value of the property.

The buyer's concerns
Alternatively, even assuming that the owner wants to improve the house's warmth, he may still have a particular need or concern for how the job is done. For example, he may have had an unfortunate experience with a previous plumber or craftsman and his main concern may therefore be to employ someone who is reliable and exact in their work. Thus, he may be particularly impressed by any written testimonials from other satisfied customers, or by the fact that the plumber had done similar work in the immediate neighbourhood. Equally, his biggest concern may be for speed: he may be worried about having his house in disarray for days on end.

Even more likely perhaps, the owner may know absolutely nothing about central-heating systems and his general instructions to Barry may easily have been no more than a hazy notion of what he thinks is required. For instance, he may be labouring under an illusion that radiators with individual heat controls are a waste of money, or that no heating system should cost more than £x.

What Barry should do
Instead of mechanically rattling off an approximate price for the job, Barry should take a few moments to clarify the owner's needs by asking a few questions along the following lines:

- Why are you thinking of having central heating?

- How familiar are you with today's systems?
- What are your main concerns?
- When exactly do you want it installed?
- Which do you prefer – saving a small amount of money on installation costs or saving a larger amount in fuel economy?

Once he knows the needs of the customer, Barry is then in a position to satisfy those needs (see below) and so give himself a reasonable chance of securing the job.

Freda stops at a garage for petrol. The owner takes her money and then asks her if, in view of the cold weather, she needs any antifreeze. As it happens, she does. And while he is getting it, she also decides to buy a scraper for her windscreen. If the garage owner had not asked whether Freda needed antifreeze, she would simply have paid for the petrol and left. Luckily, he knew the Classic Sales Method!

Joe, a mini-cab driver, has never heard of the Classic Sales Method. After taking Mr Businessman all the way to the airport very early one morning, he simply asks for the money and drives off. If only Joe had waited a moment and asked whether Mr Businessman needed a lift home from the airport upon his return, he might have secured another lucrative fare.

Abigail owns a restaurant three miles out of town. In her pre-Christmas advertising, she states that she will arrange taxis to and from the restaurant for all her diners. It is not a free service, but that is unimportant. The fact that transport is laid on in advance will go a long way towards satisfying the needs of many customers for breath-alyser-free entertainment.

Conclusion

Buyers come in a range of unique, unpredictable shapes and sizes. Some have only one need; some have two or more needs; some have no fixed idea of what their needs might be. Your job, as a sales-oriented entrepreneur, is to find out what those needs *are*. The way you do this is to *ask*.

Satisfy the needs of your buyer

Having discovered the buyer's needs, your next job is to try to satisfy them.

To do this, you must tailor the explanation of your product to the needs of the buyer. To put it another way: you must select and emphasise those details of your product that fit the particular needs of the buyer to whom you are describing it.

Product details you should know, when selling

1. If you *offer a service*, you should know precise details of:

- the general services you provide;
- any additional services;
- the costs of all services;
- discounts/payment terms;
- your reaction time;
- your back-up facilities;
- your guarantees;
- your trading history and experience;
- your local/national market position;
- type and number of clients (past/present);
- your current level of sales.

2. If you *offer a product*, you should know precise details of:

- the standard features of all your products (including dimensions, colours, functions, etc);
- any additional/optional features;
- your manufacturing/assembly processes;
- your quality assurances/safeguards;
- your product-containers and product-packaging;
- your guarantees;
- your recommended retail price;
- your trade prices/discounts/payment terms;
- your minimum order quantity;
- your 'returns' procedures;
- your point-of-sale material (if any) (shelf-stickers, posters, display racks, etc);
- your advertising support (if any);
- market research data supporting your products (if any);

- your trading history and experience;
- your local/national market position;
- type and number of clients (past/present);
- your current level of sales. **Plus:**
- you should know most of the above details in respect of any immediate competitor.

How to tailor the explanation of your product to the needs of the buyer

Although what you say will largely depend on the situation, your basic approach should be as follows:

1. Once you know the buyer's main need or concern, draw his attention to the specific details (ie, facts) that meet this need.

   For example, if the buyer's main concern is reliability, you must mention those facts that show how reliable your product is. These may include technical data on the product itself, testimonials or reports from other satisfied customers and/or third parties, details of how well the product is selling overall, and so on.

2. Having cited these facts, you must, of course, explain *how* they are likely to meet his need or alleviate his concern. In other words, you must always show how the facts and features of your product benefit the customer.

   If this sounds too obvious to be worth mentioning, let me assure you that a great many salespeople still make the mistake of droning on and on about the incredible, amazing, unique features of their products, without ever explaining how the customer will benefit.

   Always remember: customers never buy products purely because of their features or facts; customers only buy products because of the benefits those products will bring them.

   In short, telling a customer what a product will do, is never enough: you must tell him *how he will benefit as a result*.

Examples

- You are selling a new car to a customer. Having discovered that the customer is primarily interested in speed and road-handling, you must now show how the features of the car meet these two needs. You do not drone on about its spacious boot, its heated rear windows or its narrow turning circle! These three features may make the car utterly unique, but they do not benefit the customer in his search for speed and road-handling.

- You own a garden centre. You are trying to sell a plant whose only distinguishing feature is its ability to grow fast in any weather. Unfortunately, this feature is unlikely to impress anyone. However, the benefit of being able to use this plant to beautify a garden – by speedily camouflaging any ugly spots – might. You should therefore ask the customer whether his garden has/is likely to have any areas that need this sort of camouflage treatment. If he says yes (as he probably will), you can then show him how this plant will solve his problem.

- You make ceramic figures for sale to gift shops. Since most shopkeepers are consumed with the need to buy products that move off the shelves as quickly as possible, with little or no risk to themselves, it is pointless trying to impress your retail customers with your painstaking manufacturing processes and the 151 different coats of special paint which you lovingly apply to each figure. Instead, you should show your customers how buying your figures will meet their need for fast, low-risk sales. Either price your figures in such a way as to provide your customers with a large enough profit per figure to cover the risk of unsold stock, or offer a reasonable sale-or-return arrangement.

  Alternatively, provide each customer with point-of-sale material (posters/shelf-stickers/mobiles/display racks or stands) that will help to focus consumer attention on your products and so promote sales.

  As you can see, your main priority is to meet the particular needs of your customer, not to impress him with the incredibly sensational features of your product. The latter may well be of interest, but only in so far as they satisfy the former.

3. Keep your explanation concise and to the point. In particular, avoid the temptation to ramble on about other aspects of your product with which the buyer appears to be satisfied. You will only stir up a hornet's nest.

   For example, if the buyer is doubtful about your reliability, talk to him about reliability, not about price. By mentioning how cost-effective your product is, you run the risk of provoking dissent on this issue as well and as a result may have to fight on two fronts simultaneously.

Here are some more examples of how to tailor the explanation of your product to the needs of the buyer.

Examples

- You are talking to the managing director of a Midlands chain-store to whom you are trying to sell your range of handmade soft toys. Using the Classic Sales Method, you first question the buyer about his needs and discover that his main concern is the sellability of your product.

  He has already seen (and liked) a few samples of your toys and is happy with your prices; what still concerns him, however, is whether his customers are likely to want to buy cuddly crocodiles with huge teeth. In short, the need of this particular buyer is sellability.

  In order to satisfy this need, you must show how the amazing qualities of your product are likely to make it as sellable as any other soft toy, if not more so.

  Thus, your approach may go something like this:
  - Sales of your soft toys in comparable stores, in the north of England, are holding up extremely well (quote figures).
  - A market research study in London (ie, demonstrators in four stores) revealed a high level of interest (quote figures).
  - Your existing UK mail-order sales figures are increasing at a rate of . . . (quote figures).
  - These facts show that your toys are selling well throughout the country and that therefore there is no reason why they will not sell equally well in the buyer's Midland stores.

Assuming that the figures you quote are reasonably impressive, you stand a good chance of satisfying the buyer's need for sellability and making the sale.

- Alternatively, the main worry of the above toy-buyer may be product safety. He may, for instance, be concerned about the toys' inflammability or toxicity.

  In order to satisfy this concern, a slightly different approach is required. Thus, you may argue as follows:
  - EC regulations require all soft toys to conform to safety standards A, B and C.
  - All your toys have been tested by QC Co Ltd, whose final report

(which you have in your briefcase) confirms that they exceed these safety standards by a margin of x.
- This fact alone shows that the toys are perfectly safe and that therefore the buyer should have no worries.
- However, to reassure him even further, he should know that your toys have also been approved (from a safety viewpoint) by M & M – a major UK chain-store renowned for its uncompromising attitude to product safety.
- If M & M are satisfied, it is fair to conclude that the safety of your toys is beyond question.

Points

● Notice how in each example you meet the buyer's concern head on with specific facts about your toys.
● Notice you then explain *how* this information solves the buyer's need: you do not simply dump it in his lap and hope that he gets the message.
● Notice, finally, how you stick to the point throughout. No other aspect of your toys is mentioned.

Two further examples

You are a self-employed music teacher. One day, *Diana*, the mother of a five-year-old named Harry, phones you for details of your piano lessons.

Using the Classic Sales Method, you refrain from giving out any information about your piano tuition until you have found out more about Diana's needs.

As it happens, you quickly discover that she is much more interested in the snob value of having one of her children go to private music lessons than she is in the actual musical potential of little Harry.

Having discovered Diana's need for social esteem, you now proceed to satisfy it by tailoring the details of your service accordingly. Your approach may go something like this:

● You may begin by explaining your credentials, taking care to emphasise where (and under whom) you studied music. (Quote any impressive sounding names.)
● You may also give details of the names of any orchestras or ensembles with whom you play or have played.
● You may also mention the subsequent successes and/or general progress of former pupils of yours, taking care to highlight those

who prefer playing Mozart in the Albert Hall to bashing out heavy metal rhythms in basement squats!

- You may also mention the fact that, assuming Harry makes reasonable progress, he will be entered for various exams and/or recitals so as to develop his talent to the full. Emphasise that this depends on progress achieved as well as on her own parental views, but say that she would not be the first mother to have a child perform with a symphony orchestra.

- You may now confess that you personally enjoy teaching the piano not because you enjoy seeing former pupils play in the Albert Hall, but because you know you are giving your pupils a lifelong interest in a beautiful cultural activity, and (you may add) a distinctive and universally admired social skill.

- Finally, you may, should you feel the need, give precise details of your teaching methods, emphasising the time and attention you pay to each pupil's individual requirements.

- If, after any of the above points, you feel that Diana is not getting the message – that you can provide her with the social esteem that she feels she needs – you may take a moment to draw it out accordingly.

Now suppose you are the same music teacher, only this time you receive a call from *Susan*, the mother of a five-year-old named Jackie. Susan (you discover) is genuinely interested in her daughter's musical potential. In particular, being a piano-player herself (although no teacher), she shows particular interest in how you actually teach the instrument and in whether there is a danger of her daughter being pushed too hard and too fast.

Once again, having discovered your customer's main concerns, you must now proceed to satisfy them. As always, the rule is: tailor your explanation to meet the customer's concerns.

Thus, you may proceed as follows:

- Explain how pleased you are that Susan has contacted you. Tell her that she has definitely done the right thing in coming to a professional teacher while her daughter is still so young. Explain that this will enable you to take things nice and steady with Jackie and allow her to proceed entirely at her own speed.

- Emphasise that you have pupils of many different levels of ability and that your main satisfaction stems from helping each and every one of them to develop their own individual potential, regardless of any general standards.

- Tell her, therefore, that she is not to harbour the slightest worry that Jackie is in any danger of being pushed.
- Quote names of any former pupils of yours who were slow starters but who subsequently made significant strides. Tell Susan that the progress made by these pupils confirms the correctness of your patient approach to teaching music.
- Explain in detail how you go about teaching beginners like Jackie. Apart from allowing you to explain the success of your teaching methods, it also enables you to repeat how careful you are to tease out the ability of the individual slowly, without regard for general standards.

The key point: These two examples demonstrate a method of how to talk to complete strangers about your product: a method that you can practise and perfect to cope with virtually any situation. Exactly how successful it becomes, depends on your efforts!

Conclusion

Most products or services can be explained in many different ways. To satisfy your buyer's stated needs, describe your product in the way that best matches those needs.

Answer any objections

You must be fully prepared for all and any objections. They are a normal and natural feature of any sales process involving human beings. Not only are most human beings understandably sceptical about parting with money, they are also wary of accepting the word of any salesperson without argument.

When objections are raised by the buyer, your job is to listen to them carefully and then answer them in such a way as to reassure the buyer that your product is, at least, *worth taking a risk with*. To do this, use the following method.

The Welcome-Probe-Test-Answer method

Welcome

The first thing you should do when a buyer raises an objection is to *welcome* it. For example, say something like:

'I'm glad you mentioned that' or
'Yes, I agree, that's an important issue.'

This approach pays off straightaway. Not only does it help to reduce the tension and put the buyer at ease, it also allows you to regain the initiative. After all, by actually welcoming his objection, you show that you are not in the least bit worried about being able to answer it. This confidence alone will have a positive effect on your listener.

Probe

Having welcomed the buyer's objection, you should now ask one or two open questions in order to *probe* for the extent of his concern. Depending on the issue raised, say something like:

'Can you explain that a little bit more for me?' or
'Can you be a little more precise?' or
'What level of reliability are you looking for?' or
'What sort of features were you hoping for?' or
'When you say that the product is too expensive, what exactly do you mean?' or
'What exactly do you mean when you say it's not really your sort of product?'

The reason for this probing is simple: how can you answer an objection properly before knowing the extent of that objection?

Test

Even after you have welcomed the objection and probed for clarification, you should still refrain from answering it until you have *tested* it. Why? Because buyers frequently hide their real concerns behind a smokescreen of lesser objections.

In other words, the visible objection – the one that you think is the real one – may simply be a cover for another more serious concern. If you rush into answering a fake objection you will waste time, achieve nothing and inevitably lose the initiative.

Test with an if-question

Depending on the nature of the objection raised, test it by asking a question along the following lines:

'If I can show you that my product is at least as reliable as the ones

you are using at the moment, will that satisfy you?'
'If I can demonstrate that my product is likely to appeal to more
people than the one you've been using up until now, will that
convince you to buy it?'
'If I show you two different testimonials from companies similar in
size and operation to yours, will that reassure you about my company record?'
'If I can show you two ways in which my company's service is
actually better than the companies you currently use, will that
persuade you to give us a try?'

Faced with a question of this sort, the buyer is almost certain to react
in one of two ways: either he will say Yes – in which case you can
then proceed to answer the objection – or else he will hum and ha for
a few moments before admitting his real worry – in which case you
must repeat the Welcome/Probe/Test procedure and then answer it.

Answer

Most objections concern standard matters such as competence, reliability, delivery, after-sales service or back-up, price, payment terms,
and overall convenience. They can therefore be anticipated – and
their answers prepared – well in advance.

When preparing your answers, your basic aim should be to convince all sceptics that your product is *worth taking a risk with*.

Push for the order

This is the focal point of the sales process: the moment when – having explained the relevant benefits of your product and answered any
objections – you push the buyer into buying your product.

The four best closes

In the sales world, this pushing exercise is known as closing or the
close: ie, the stage at which you close the sale and get the order. There
are dozens of different closes; the one you choose will normally
depend on *how your conversation with the buyer is going*. We shall
look at four of the most useful, as follows:

● The Alternative Close

- The Assumptive Close
- The Incentive Close
- The What-on-Earth Close.

The Alternative Close

This works well in nearly all situations where you are offering a range of products and where you are not encountering too much resistance from your buyer.

The point of the Alternative Close is that, instead of asking the buyer whether, for example, he wants your *red* product, you ask him *which* product he wants – the red or the green one. Obviously, whichever he chooses, he ends up buying something and hey presto you have closed the sale!

This may sound a trifle forward or impudent, but believe me, it works. Some buyers actually visibly relax once you have taken the responsibility, of *whether* to buy, off their shoulders, thus leaving them the less stressful task of choosing *which particular* product suits them best.

Example

You own a garage. A motorist turns up at the counter with an enquiry.

> *Buyer:* Can you tell me the cost of your new batteries?
> *You:* I sell two types: the Dalek one is £30 and the Krypton is £40. I've got both in stock, which one do you want?

A good example of how to conjure up an almost certain sale from what may be a simple enquiry.

The Assumptive Close

This works well when the product in question is clearly defined and when your only problem is a buyer who dithers.

You employ it by simply assuming that the buyer is going to buy and by proceeding to talk about the mechanical details of the assumed order.

Example

You have a removals company and you are on the phone to a customer who is dithering about whether to use your service.

> *Buyer:* Yes ... hmnn ... I'm not sure ...

You: Well at this stage, Mr Smith, I think I'd better put you down for one of our lorries or else you're going to miss out completely. Now when is the best time for us to call? Would 8am be too early?

The Incentive Close

This works well in nearly all selling situations where your overall presentation has gone well but where, once again, your buyer is reluctant to commit himself.

As the name suggests, this close is based upon offering the buyer a tangible incentive to complete the deal on the spot. Usually, the incentive is money off the purchase price, although it may also be a free sample of goods, an additional special service or even a personal gift.

The trick about this close is to appear to give away as much as possible while actually having to part with very little.

Example

You own a stationery distribution company. You are trying to persuade a buyer to give you an order for six boxes of computer stationery. The date is 1 February.

Buyer: It all sounds OK, but I'd rather have a think about it.
You: OK, well look, give me the order for the six boxes now and I'll throw in our last carton of desk diaries for nothing. How's that?

On the face of it, a simple case of giving away something for nothing. In fact, not only have you been given the diaries by another company as a promotional gift, but you also deliberately avoid mentioning how many diaries are in the carton. It may be 50; it may be five.

The What-on-Earth Close

This close is designed as a fall-back to all the others and should only be used as a last-ditch attempt to salvage your sale from certain oblivion. Ironically, despite its dire context, it is a perfectly sensible and plausible way for you to push for the order and works more often than you think.

Use it when dealing with Mr Just-Won't-Make-Up-His-Mind-Whatever-You-Say, ie, when the buyer seems to be impervious to all your arguments for no good reason. Say something like this:

- I have listened carefully to your requirements.
- I have shown you how my product meets those requirements.
- I have listened carefully to your objections.
- I have done a reasonable job of answering those objections and have demonstrated that the risk to you and your company, in buying my product, is minimal.
- What, therefore, is the problem? Or, to put it another way, what do I have to do to convince you?

At the very least, the buyer should open up a bit and explain what's bugging him. Of course, by telling you his real concern, he thereby hands you the opportunity of repeating the whole Welcome/Probe/Test/Close procedure all over again!

How to get the most out of the Classic Sales Method

Like any method of selling, the Classic Sales Method is far from foolproof. Nevertheless, as its name suggests, it is a universally accepted way of selling most products and services to most people. Customise it, adapt it to your particular business, but have confidence in it: it *works*!

The right mental attitude to selling

In order to sell more, not only do you need to stick to a reliable sales method, you also need to adopt the right attitude.

After all, you are planning to persuade a number of complete strangers to buy your product – a product they may never have sampled or seen before. Furthermore, these strangers may be highly sceptical of what you say and, in many cases, are likely to reject your proposals.

Unless you are mentally prepared for this rejection, it can easily cause you to lose faith either in your product or yourself or both, with correspondingly fatal consequences for your business.

How to maintain the right mental attitude

This is not a book on sales psychology so I will confine myself to offering you the following simple tips:

How to maintain the right mental attitude

This is not a book on sales psychology so I will confine myself to offering you the following simple tips:

In general, assume the best but prepare for the worst

In other words, always assume that you and your product are as good as any other combination, *but*, at the same time, assume that others will initially disagree. Mentally prepare yourself accordingly.

Appreciate the real meaning of 'No'

It is perfectly natural for customers to reject your initial proposals and say No. Why? Because customers are just as lazy as anyone else. They often say No simply to avoid having to act. Indeed, very few customers who say No actually mean No. Instead they mean one of the following:

1. Not really; 2. Not today; 3. Not now; 4. Not sure; 5. Not convinced; 6. Not bothered; 7. Not at that price; 8. Not buying anything this week; 9. Not in the mood; 10. Not usually something we buy; 11. Not enough time to think; 12. Not unless you push it; 13. Not familiar enough with you/your product; 14. Not ready; 15. Not my responsibility; 16. Not in the least bit interested; 17. Not in the middle of a meeting.

Note that not one of these responses is a genuine or a considered rejection of your product.

The moral is: never get despondent when a customer says No. He may really mean something quite different.

Remove the unknown in selling

In my experience, most of the mental stress suffered by salespeople is caused by uncertainty or fear of the unknown.

For example, you pick up the phone to call a customer for the first time. What will you say? What happens if you disturb him in the middle of a meeting? What if he bites your head off? What happens if you dry up and forget what to say?

All these questions flash through your mind as you wait for your connection. And if the worst happens (as it sometimes does) and you *do* dry up, you are naturally reluctant to try again for fear of repeating the experience.

The best way of reducing (and ultimately eliminating) this uncertainty or fear of the unknown is to *remove the unknown*! You must pre-plan everything so thoroughly that, no matter what happens, you know exactly what to do and how to do it.

For example, try the following:

- Write out all the possible responses that a customer can make to whatever you are proposing.
- Next to each response, write your own reply: ie, the points you should make in order to reassure the customer.
- Practise saying all this aloud. If necessary, role-play the whole scene with a partner or friend.
- To give yourself extra confidence, keep a series of written notes to hand, to remind you of what to say whenever you speak to a customer over the phone.

In case you think that all this sounds rather contrived and amateurish: think again. Meticulous preparation and pre-planning are the hallmarks of most of the world's greatest entrepreneurs.

The Classic Sales Method – Conclusion

No matter what you sell or who you sell it to, you can depend upon the Classic Sales Method. The remainder of this book shows you how to apply this method of selling to your business.

2

Sell more by organising yourself properly

This is your first step towards sales success. It is the foundation for everything that follows, so read this chapter carefully.

Why organise yourself?

Small businesses lose more sales through being disorganised than for any other reason. Why? Because too many entrepreneurs regard organisation as a fundamentally unproductive activity. In fact, the reverse is true. To be organised means working to a clear set of *priorities*. It means concentrating all your efforts and resources on what is *important* to you and your business.

How to organise yourself

Your best approach is to adopt the following sequence:

- *Stop* and find out the facts of your business.
- *Decide* on a new sales plan.

Stop and find out the facts of your business

This is the very first step you must take. It is usually painful but always essential. Too many entrepreneurs live and work in blissful ignorance of the *exact* details of their business. This may be tolerable when business is booming but catastrophic when it is not.

'*I don't have time.*' This is the usual excuse that most entrepreneurs make to themselves for remaining ignorant. They refuse to make time and, all too often, suffer the consequences. So, do yourself a favour: stop for a moment and find out what is really happening to your business. If you do not have time: *make time*.

What you need to know about your business

- *Exactly what you are selling*
  By type – eg, 24 × blue, 75 × red, 91 × violet, etc.
  By value – eg, £480 worth of blue, £750 worth of red, etc.
- *To whom you are selling it*
  List all customers and their respective purchases/discounts.
- *How much gross profit these sales generate*
  From your product sales deduct the cost of those products and
  also any other specific costs related to their sale. For example, you
  sell each blue for £20 and buy it for £10. But each blue is sold by
  mail-order and postage is £1.50 per sale. Thus, profit on blues is
  £8.50 × 24 = £204. Do the same for all your other products.
- *What it costs to sell to and to service your customers*
  Make an assessment of the extra costs involved in dealing with certain types of customer. For example, if a chain-store buys £1000 of
  your products each month and requires an extra 5 per cent discount for doing so, this customer is costing you an extra £50 to
  sell to. If, in addition, you spend £50 a week taking his buyer out
  to lunch, the customer is costing an extra £200 a month to service:
  ie, total extra costs of £250.

What you should discover

From the above figures, you should try to establish the following:

- Which products are the best and worst sellers.
- Which products are the most and least profitable.
- How many customers you sell to.
- Which customers buy the most and the least.
- Which customers make you the most and the least profit.

Costs and cashflow – what you need to know

Sales pay costs. The higher your costs, the higher your sales must be.
Do not, therefore, ignore the financial side of things. What is the
point of striving hard to boost sales, only to see the benefits wiped
out by financial mismanagement? To avoid this, try to find out most of
the following information:

- *How much you have to pay out in costs each week/month*
  Itemised as follows:

- Rent
- Total cost of employees (PAYE/NI, wages, overtime, etc)
- All hire-purchase costs (cars, other equipment, etc)
- Admin costs (telephone, electricity, stationery, postage).

● *Details of any outstanding suppliers' bills*
ie, important bills that must be settled in order to maintain your business.

● *How much money is owed to you by your customers*
Itemised as follows:
- Details of debts that are so old or in such dispute that they are unlikely, in practice, ever to be collected.
- Which customers and what sums are more than two months overdue; and what is the customer's explanation for this.
- The approximate amount you can expect to be paid by customers over (say) the next two months.

What you should discover

From the above information, you should be able to establish:

● How secure your cash position is, and which is more important: collecting debts to pay your bills or generating new sales.
● How much you have to sell over (say) the next two months to stay in business.
● How you stand with your important suppliers.

Conclusion – knowing this information puts you in control

These figures may or may not come as a surprise to you. The point is that you now know the *facts* of your business. You are now in control. You can therefore make plans and take decisions on the basis of fact rather than fantasy.

Decide on a new sales plan

A sales plan is simply a large sheet of paper containing your own estimate of how many of each product you will sell (at what price and at what cost) week by week or month by month, for a period of one year.

Why make a sales plan? Two vital reasons

First, it forces you to think about your business and especially your sales operation.

For example, in order to estimate your future sales, you must consider, for example, what extra customers you are likely to win, or whether it is worth while hiring an extra salesperson, or whether your prices need to be raised or lowered, or what extra resources are required (such as a higher bank overdraft facility), and so on.

Second, by reducing your business to a set of dispassionate digits, it allows you (or your bank manager) to see exactly how the business is performing at any time during the year, and take appropriate action.

How to make a sales plan

1. Take a sheet of A4 paper; across the top, write the months of the year, beginning with the next month.
2. Down the left-hand side of the sheet, write out a list of all your *products* (ie, the goods or services that you sell). Next to each product, write its average net sale price to your customers.
3. Estimate how many of *each product* you are likely to sell, month by month, over the next 12 months: put your monthly estimate for each product in the column under the month concerned. (See 'How to estimate sales' below.)
4. Next to each estimate of the *number* of products you think will sell, write its *monetary value*.

Example

A simple, three-monthly sales plan for a new greeting-card business, selling four different types of greeting card to shops, might read as follows:

Product details	Jan	Feb	Mar
Sales			
Birthday cards (Average sale price £1) Number sold/@ £ value	400/£400	500/£500	600/£600
Special occasion cards (Average sale price 90p) Number sold/@ £ value	200/£180	200/£180	300/£270
Amusing blank cards (Average sale price 80p) Number sold/@ £ value	180/£144	180/£144	250/£200
Valentine cards (Average sale price £1.20) Number sold/ @ £ value	1600/£1920	800/£960	Nil
Total sales = A	**£2644.00**	**£1784.00**	**£1070.00**

Thus, underneath these monthly sales estimates, write the monetary value of their costs.

For example, the costs section of the card company's sales plan may look something like this.

Your sales plan now contains a clear breakdown of sales and the costs of those sales. To complete matters, simply subtract your

Product details	Jan	Feb	Mar
Costs			
Birthday cards (Average cost 35p) Number sold/@ £ cost	400/£140	500/£175	600/£210
Special occasion cards (Average cost 40p) Number sold/@ £ cost	200/£80	200/£80	300/£120
Amusing blank cards (Average cost 20p) Number sold/@ £ cost	180/£36	180/£36	250/£50
Valentine cards (Average cost 50p) Number sold/ @ £ cost	1600/£800	800/£400	Nil
Total costs = B	**£1056.00**	**£691.00**	**£380.00**

Your sales plan now contains a clear breakdown of sales and the costs of those sales. To complete matters, simply subtract your monthly costs from your monthly sales. The resulting figure is your monthly gross profit.

For example, when the figure for gross profit is added, the complete three-monthly sales plan of our card company looks like this:

Product details	Jan	Feb	Mar
Sales			
Birthday cards (Average sale price £1) Number sold/@ £ value	400/£400	500/£500	600/£600
Special occasion cards (Average sale price 90p) Number sold/@ £ value	200/£180	200/£180	300/£270
Amusing blank cards (Average sale price 80p) Number sold/@ £ value	180/£144	180/£144	250/£200
Valentine cards (Average sale price £1.20) Number sold/ @ £ value	1600/£1920	800/£960	Nil
Total sales = A	£2644.00	£1784.00	£1070.00
Costs			
Birthday cards (Average cost 35p) Number sold/@ £ cost	400/£140	500/£175	600/£210
Special occasion cards (Average cost 40p) Number sold/@ £ cost	200/£80	200/£80	300/£120
Amusing blank cards (Average cost 20p) Number sold/@ £ cost	180/£36	180/£36	250/£50
Valentine cards (Average cost 50p) Number sold/ @ £ cost	1600/£800	800/£400	Nil
Total costs = B	£1056.00	£691.00	£380.00
Gross profit (A – B) =	£1588.00	£1093.00	£690.00

The most important feature of a sales plan

The above sales plan looks very pretty, you may say; but how does the owner of the company *know* what is going to happen? For instance, how does he know that 1600 Valentine cards are going to be sold in January? The answer is, he doesn't.

The above sales plan – like all sales plans – is no more than a series of *assumptions* (informed guesses) about what will happen. Indeed, as we shall now see, the most important feature of a sales plan is not so much the actual figures inside it, as the *reasoning* behind it.

How to estimate sales

Estimating sales is not a matter of plucking figures out of thin air or of simply writing down what you instinctively feel will happen. This approach is no good to anyone. Instead, carefully consider all the facts, together with any/all information that may have an impact on your business.

For example, you should take into account the following:

- The number of customers you currently sell to.
- The number of additional customers you can expect to sell to.
- The average order size of these customers.
- The number of new products you can expect to sell to them.
- Any additional sales resources you are likely to acquire.
- Any expected rise/fall in your average selling prices.
- Any expected rise/fall in your average cost of sales.
- Seasonal selling advantages (eg, increased demand at Christmas).
- Seasonal selling disadvantages (eg, post-Christmas slump).
- Any expected increase/decrease in competition.
- Any other factors that are likely to affect what you sell or how you sell it.

Based upon this known information, you then make a series of reasonable *assumptions* as to what is likely to happen to your sales over (say) the next 12 months.

To take a very simple example, if you are a window cleaner, your approach to making a sales plan may go something like this:

- First, you may work out that your weekly round includes a total of 100 cleaning jobs for 50 shops/offices and 50 houses. Since you charge £2.50 per job your total weekly sales are £250.

Other relevant facts you consider may include: the fact that your present charge (having remained the same for the past two years) is due for a rise, and the fact that several shops have asked whether you would clean their windows twice a week, but at a reduced rate.

- Second, based upon this information, you make the following reasonable assumptions:
  - You assume an increase in your charge to £2.75p.
  - You assume that 30 per cent of your present shop/office customers will agree to have their windows cleaned twice a week, at a reduced rate of £2.
- Calculating the effect of these assumptions, you find that your 50 house customers now give you a weekly income of £137.50p (instead of the previous £125); 35 of your shop/office customers now give a weekly income of £96.25p (instead of the previous £87.50p), and 15 give a weekly income of £60 (instead of the previous £37.50p).

Thus, on the basis of these assumptions, your weekly sales estimate for the next 12 months is £293.75 – an increase of 17.5 per cent or £43.75p on your previous £250 per week.

- One drawback, however, is the fact that you will now have to clean 15 extra windows per week. In effect, this reduces your average charge per window from £2.75p to £2.55p.

Points

- Notice how you first gather your facts and then use them to arrive at your assumptions as to what is likely to happen.
- Notice that, if challenged as to how you think you are likely to increase sales by 17.5 per cent, you can justify yourself by reference to your assumptions. Any discussion of your new sales estimates will therefore focus on the accuracy of these assumptions, rather than on the strength of your gut feelings or business instincts.

How to estimate sales – a summary

1. Gather together as much information as possible about your intended sales operation and what might affect it.
2. Ask yourself: On the basis of this information, what assumptions can I reasonably make about what will happen to my sales?

3. Calculate your estimates and draw up your sales plan accordingly.
4. Write out your assumptions and add them to the end of your plan. Remember, these assumptions represent the vital reasoning behind the plan.

Example

The new greeting-card company, whose sales plan was outlined above, is owned by *Horatio*. In order to arrive at his sales estimates for January, February and March, Horatio first considers all the facts, then makes his assumptions, as follows:

Horatio starts with the *facts*:

- He has a list of 1000 potential customers, divided into three different types of outlet: newsagents, independent specialist card shops and others (including garages, post offices, etc).
- He has already mailed details of his cards to each of these 1000 customers and has followed up this mailshot with telephone calls to 50 customers from each type of outlet (ie, a total of 150 calls).
- From enquiries received in answer to his mailshot, and from talking to customers over the phone, Horatio feels confident that his cards will receive a *reasonable response* from the trade, especially his Valentine cards whose original and amusing designs were praised by several different customers.
- Regarding product details, each of his cards is available in five different designs and he intends selling them in packs of ten (ie, each pack comprises ten cards, two each of the five designs).
- He has already fixed the sale price of his cards by reference to the prices of other card suppliers, but before entering them on to his sales plan he deducts an average shop discount of 40 per cent from each sale price, in accordance with standard practice.
- He has fairly large stocks of each card and thus is free to devote himself exclusively to sales for the first three months. Although he intends to do most of his selling by phone, he also plans a number of personal visits to certain customers.
- To aid his sales efforts, he has bought a stock of swivel display stands that he intends to offer (free of charge) to any of the larger card shops that buy his cards. He expects to offer these stands to the customers he visits in person.

Horatio next makes his *assumptions*.

For example, his January sales figures for Valentine cards (1600 cards) are based upon the following assumptions:

- He assumes that, in January, he will make an average of ten telephone calls per hour, for an average of eight hours a day, five days a week. (A wee bit optimistic!)
- He assumes that in 40 of these 80 calls, he will be able to speak to the shop-owner or buyer. (This is reasonable.)
- He assumes that of these 40 buyers, roughly one in ten will be persuaded to buy a pack of Valentine cards. This will give him daily sales of four packs (40 cards).
- In turn, this means monthly (20 working days) sales of 80 packs (800 cards): ie, half his planned sales. (Given the time of year and the type of product, this seems reasonable.)
- He further assumes that, one day a week, he will personally visit buyers in eight larger shops. With the added carrot of a free display stand, he reckons to sell an average of five packs to four out of these eight buyers: ie, 20 packs per week or 800 cards per month. (This is a little optimistic.)

Important safety features of any sales plan

Every sales plan should, in my opinion, contain a few safety features along the following lines:

- Err on the conservative side when estimating sales.
- Err on the pessimistic side when estimating costs.

Notice that our hero, Horatio, makes no assumption as to repeat sales. This is not because he believes that no one is likely to re-order: far from it. He merely prefers to have this benefit up his sleeve, as a safety factor, to offset any shortfall in his planned sales.

To write, change or update your sales plan – use a computer

I said earlier, when explaining how to make a sales plan, that you should use a sheet of A4 paper. This may be the way you begin, but I strongly recommend that you transfer your figures on to a computer as soon as possible.

If you do not have a computer, look up Computer Services or Secretarial Services in your *Yellow Pages* and arrange for your sales

No sales plan is like the ten commandments

No sales plan is written in stone or must be obeyed for eternity. A sales plan is only as good as the assumptions underlying it. Therefore, if its assumptions change: change the plan! A plan should always reflect your best estimate of what is realistically achievable, not simply what you would like to happen.

When should you start your new sales plan?

As soon as you have finished reading this book! You can read more about budgeting and cash flow forecasts in *Budgeting for Business* and *Cash Flow And How To Improve It*, both by Leon Hopkins and published by Kogan Page.

3

Sell more by injecting real sales power into your business routines

This is your second step towards sales success. Start increasing your sales by sharpening up your day-to-day business procedures.

Make it easy for customers to contact you

The easier it is for customers to contact you, the more sales you will make. Remember: one of the biggest causes of lost sales is an engaged telephone.

Make sure you have more than enough phone lines

As a rule of thumb, you should always have one more line than you actually need. ·

Most businesses need a fax machine

If you sell to other businesses then a fax machine is *vital*; if you sell only to the general public, it may still prove an excellent investment. For example, it can speed up your buying, or save you time by allowing you to fax purchase orders to your suppliers overnight.

Sell more by using an answerphone

The only way to appreciate the true value of an answerphone is to be on the end of an unanswered phone when you are desperate to leave an important message.

Most types will store messages for you and then replay them to you when you telephone. So, if your phone is in London, your customer is in Tokyo and you are in Cape Town, your customer can dial your number and leave a message that the answerphone will replay for your ears when you telephone a little later. There is no longer any need to let geographical remoteness or physical absence interrupt your sales!

Mobile phones – to have or have not?

For some entrepreneurs a mobile phone is essential. Equally, for others it is no more than a pointless extravagance. How can you assess its usefulness to you?

To begin with, you should establish a mobile phone's true cost. Suppose, for example, its brand-new price is £250 and its line charges and premium call charges add up to an extra £1500 per annum. What are you getting for your money?

Subject to the occasional technical hitch, the answer is two things. First, you become instantly contactable by all your customers – at least by those who have your number. Second, you are able to dispense with the need for a full-time receptionist because you are now in a position to do that job yourself!

Thus, your decision to buy a mobile phone boils down to this: is instant availability and the saving of the cost of a receptionist worth, for example, £1750 to you in the first year?

Sell more by learning how to answer the phone effectively

Very few entrepreneurs make the most of their initial contact with customers. This is usually because they are disorganised and unprepared. Try to avoid this mistake.

Remember, for example, that you will not always answer your own telephone. It may be a member of your staff, a secretary or even your wife. Do not leave the efficiency of your business to someone who is unprepared. Follow these simple tips:

Have your customer enquiry forms next to the phone

The number one rule of answering customer enquiries is: get the customer's name, his telephone number, his enquiry and (if possible) his address. Without this information you will never be able to re-contact or sell to this customer in the future.

Because you will usually have only a few moments of the caller's time, make your own customer enquiry forms and keep them next to the phone for *anyone who answers the phone* to use.

Ideally, your form should include the following headings: *name, address, telephone number, action required*, plus any other relevant headings that may prompt you (or whoever answers the phone) to ask important questions, for example, *when to ring customer*.

Your product information sheet

Some customers demand a precise answer to their enquiry. To facilitate and impress this type of customer, make sure you have a written list of relevant information, next to the phone, to quote from.

Your personal availability diary

Sometimes customers need to see you personally. Make it easy for them! Always keep an up-to-date account of your movements, next to the phone, to avoid the necessity of having to call the customer back. An appointment left hanging can easily become an appointment lost.

Customer complaint calls

Customers with complaints need careful handling. In line with the Classic Sales Method, I recommend the following approach:

1. Thank (yes, thank!) the customer for drawing your attention to his complaint: you want all your customers to be 100 per cent satisfied. Take his name, address, telephone number, etc. Enter these details on to your customer enquiry form.
2. Ask him to explain why he is dissatisfied, then shut up and listen. Do not interrupt the customer, even when he starts to talk complete nonsense.
3. If necessary, clarify the exact details of the complaint by repeating them back to the customer.
4. Answer the main point of the complaint. If the customer is entitled to return his purchase or receive a refund, never explain this to him without, at the same time, emphasising your commitment to 100 per cent customer satisfaction. Always make a virtue out of a necessity.

5. Your final task is to suggest what the customer should do. If the customer does not accept your advice, arrange to see him or phone him back. Only as a last resort should you tell him to take it or leave it. This approach rarely succeeds in encouraging repeat business.

Customer sales enquiries

In line with the Classic Sales Method, do the following:

1. *Thank the customer for calling.*
   If feasible, ask how he found out about your company.
2. *Ask him for his details*
   If necessary, make up some excuse about having trouble with your phone line; you need his name and phone number in case he is accidentally cut off.

   You ask for this information immediately, both to keep the caller talking, and also in case you forget to ask for it at the end. Incidentally, any customer who prefers not to give his name, etc is not worth worrying about.
3. *Ask how you can help, then listen.*
   In particular, listen for the customer's *need*.
4. *Clarify the customer's need by asking questions*
   In other words, you diplomatically quiz him about what he has just told you, in order to find out how best to respond.

   - Thus, for example, if a customer rings to say he is interested in buying a particular product (which you may or may not have in stock) clarify his need by asking questions such as:
     - What exactly do you want it for?
     - How familiar are you with this sort of product?
     - How soon do you need it?
     - What alternatives have you considered?
     - If I were to show you a different one that was better value and did the job just as well, how would you feel about it?
   - Alternatively, if the customer is interested in a particular service (which you may or may not provide), put questions such as:
     - What exactly do you want to achieve?
     - What exactly is your problem?
     - How often does this situation tend to arise?
     - How urgent is the situation?

- If I were to show you a different but equally effective way of solving the problem, how would you feel?

5. *Satisfy the customer's need*
   In other words, tailor your explanation of your product/service to suit the particular need of the enquirer. This does not mean that you should bend the truth! Simply emphasise those benefits of your product/service that seem to match the customer's own needs.

6. *Recommend your customer to act*
   At the end of every telephone sales enquiry, you should recommend your customer to act. *Never allow a customer simply to ring off!* For example, depending on the situation, you should recommend one of the following:

- *Suggest that he buys*
  If possible, close the sale immediately.
- *Suggest that he visits your premises to buy*
  Arrange a specific time and be there to finalise matters.
- *Suggest that you visit him to finalise the sale*
  Then arrange an appointment immediately: ideally for the following day.
- *Suggest that he places an immediate order for the product*
  Do this even when the product in question is out of stock to stop the customer looking elsewhere.
- *Suggest that he postpones any firm decision until you ring back*
  Use this approach when you need to verify certain matters. Then arrange a specific, convenient time to call back.

7. *The 'Incidentally . . .' signing-off technique*
   Whatever happens during stages 1–6, you will invariably have one final sales opportunity. Before saying goodbye, say something like:

- Incidentally, before I go, is there anything else you might be interested in? For example, how are you fixed for X, Y, Z?
- Incidentally, before I go, how often do you need X, Y, Z?
- Incidentally, before I go, may I just ask:
  - How often do you look for X, Y, Z?
  - What sort of price do you normally pay for X, Y, Z?
  - Who is the person in your company who usually buys your X, Y, Z?
  - I have a few excellent X, Y, Z; would you like to try one?

All these last-minute questions are asked to establish additional customer needs or to elicit important information for future use. Since the customer is not usually on his guard at this eleventh hour, you stand a good chance of either selling him something extra, or of obtaining some useful sales information.

Sell more by making the most of your face-to-face enquiries

Many of the above rules and suggestions also apply to face-to-face customer contact.

Whenever possible, get the customer's personal details

At the risk of repeating myself, you cannot sell to anyone unless you know who they are and how to contact them. Thus, whenever you are approached by a customer in person, you should make every effort to obtain his personal details and phone number.

Examples

Cynthia runs a second-hand bookshop. Before any customer leaves the shop – irrespective of whether they have bought a book or not – she asks them what sort of book(s) they are interested in.

Having made a note of the details of their reply on paper (in front of them), she then explains that she often has such books in stock – but often only for a few days – and suggests that she takes the customer's phone number and contacts him the next time she has any books of interest.

Result? Cynthia now has a growing mailing list of interested book-buyers which she uses both to publicise her latest literary acquisitions and to shape her buying policies.

Anne runs a series of weekly slimming classes in two small market towns. At the beginning of each 12-week class, she asks each slimmer to fill out a registration form with details of their name, address and phone number; she does the same with anyone who joins the class at a later stage.

Result? Anne has a comprehensive mailing list of all her past and present class-members through which she advertises her new classes and sells an expanding range of slimming products. Because of this list, her promotional costs have shrunk to almost nothing.

Moses runs a household electrical shop in the high street. To take full advantage of his customer contact, Moses operates a free monthly prize-draw. Any customer entering the shop is encouraged to leave his personal details (together with the nature of his enquiry) by completing a very brief free prize-draw form.

Alternatively, a customer is told that the shop regularly sends out a bargain catalogue to all its customers. In this case, the customer fills out a special bargain catalogue form.

Result? Moses has a valuable list of local customers plus details of their enquiries. Three times a year, everyone on the list receives either a mail-order brochure or a bargain catalogue of Moses' latest offers, plus information on Moses' emergency repair service. In addition, by consulting his list and the dates of the various product enquiries, Moses can form an impression of how demand changes over the year. This helps him to decide when and how many of each product to order from his suppliers.

Sell more by creating the right impression

A young man with torn jeans and spiky hair creates a very different impression from that of a young man in a suit and short back and sides. What we think is often conditioned by what we see. This applies to companies as much as to people.

Make sure your business stationery creates the right impression

What exactly is the right impression? Obviously, it depends on the nature of your business. If you own a small, luxury restaurant, your main aim may be to convey an aura of quality. By contrast, if you run a pizza delivery service, your priority may be to create an impression of action and speed.

A good way to determine the right image for you is to ask yourself, 'If I was one of my customers, what sort of qualities would I look for in a company like mine?'

How to impress the eye of the buyer

Having selected the appropriate image, you must now create it.

- *A company logo/symbol* is the most powerful and effective means of creating a particular image. If nothing else, a logo gives your company its own unique identity and makes it stand out. Ideally, ask a commercial artist to design something that is visually relevant to your business, and avoid anything too subtle. For instance, if the logo can actually depict one of the benefits you offer to customers, so much the better.

- *A company caption or message* is another aid to creating the right impression. For example, the caption

  'The Company that Guarantees Everything it Sells'

  draws immediate attention to the benefit on offer.
- *Borders* are an optional extra. They can distract as well as attract attention, so take care to subordinate them to your overall design.
- *The typeface* used on your company name and address, etc should also be appropriate. Some typefaces are more angular and loud; others are quieter and more solid-looking. Choose the type and size that fits best with your overall desired image.
- *Colours make a difference.* Bright colours (bright red, blue, green or yellow) are strident, attention-grabbing colours, ideal for creating impressions of action/speed/power, etc. By contrast, softer colours (beige, silver, rich yellow, dark blue or green, burgundy) convey quality and reliability. Once again, choose the type that fits best.
- *Paper also talks.* Generally speaking, the more expensive the paper, the more it says luxury and quality. Thus, if these qualities are important to your business, use a more expensive paper. Otherwise, use a cheaper brand. Avoid dark paper colours: they do not photocopy well.
- *Use a wordprocessor or typewriter, never a human hand.* Never write a business letter by hand. Ideally, invest in a wordprocessor. (See 'Wordprocessing your business' on page 56.) If using a typewriter, use one with an automatic correction facility. This saves you having to despatch letters cratered with correction fluid.
- *Never, never, never, sign and send a business letter without reading it first.* Need I say more? Try impressing a buyer whose name you have misspelt and you will see what I mean.

How to pack real sales power into your sales brochure

A sales brochure is a vital weapon in your sales armoury. It creates an impression of your business, it explains why a customer should buy from you and tells him how to do it. Even more important, a sales brochure is *written* and its sales message, once read, is less likely to be *forgotten*.

A verbal sales presentation, by contrast, is rarely remembered by anyone. According to experts, we forget nearly 80 per cent of what we hear within 24 hours!

The five vital questions that every sales brochure must answer

Every brochure *must* answer the following questions:

1. *What* specific benefits will a customer receive from buying your product and/or dealing with your company?
2. *How* does your product/company provide these benefits?
3. *What* proof do you have for your claims?
4. *To what extent* do you minimise the risk of buying your product?
5. *What action* should the customer take once he has read the brochure?

Question 1. Explain your benefits

- Think about the principal aspects or features of your product.
- In each case ask the question: So what? or, How will a customer benefit from this particular feature?
- Arrange these customer benefits in order of importance.
- As a guide, put yourself in the position of a typical customer who is likely to buy your product and ask yourself: What are my principal needs/concerns when buying this sort of product?
- Your brochure should highlight the benefits of your product that meet these needs.

Example

Boris owns a small building company whose main business is building extensions/converting attics/general domestic repair work. He believes that his customers' main needs or concerns are: reliability/competence; convenience/avoiding mess; and cost.

Accordingly, his sales brochure emphasises how reliable, how careful and how cost-effective his building work is.

Question 2. Explain how you deliver these benefits

- Consider each benefit in turn. Ask yourself: What features of my product or company provide or justify this benefit?
- Be as specific as possible.

Example

In his sales brochure, *Boris* the builder justifies each of his benefits, in turn, by means of the following:

Reliable and competent work:

- By carefully explaining (using text and diagrams) how his company approaches two typical building jobs and what different stages are involved: for example, planning/preparation/building, etc. An approximate time-scale is outlined for each stage.
- By showing a series of impressive before-and-after photographs of previous work, complete with captions explaining precisely the planning/preparation/building/finishing work involved.
- By quoting testimonial letters from satisfied customers.
- By quoting letters of reference from, for example, the local council planning office.
- By giving precise details of his building guarantee.
- By citing:
    - His company's 12 years' trading experience.
    - His company's membership of X Building Federation.
    - His membership of the Federation of Master Builders.

Convenient and careful work:

- By quoting testimonial letters from satisfied customers that testify to the company's flexibility in fitting in with the domestic requirements of the customer.
- By explaining (with the aid of drawings/photographs) the specific measures taken by the company to minimise mess and disruption.

Cost-effectiveness:

- By demonstrating how certain building improvements add value to the property concerned. This is illustrated with references to actual work done by the company, complete with photographs.
- This last point is further supported by a quote from an official spokesperson of, for example, the Association of Estate Agents and Valuers that acknowledges the financial benefit of home building improvements.

- By quoting testimonial letters from customers testifying to the reasonableness of the company's charges and to the value for money offered by the company.

Note. Boris never includes any prices in his sales brochure.

- He believes that there is no advantage in publicising prices, unless they are the lowest in town. They will only succeed in scaring away customers.
- In his experience, building jobs are notoriously difficult to price in advance.
- By not broadcasting his prices in advance he remains free to charge what he feels is appropriate in each case.
- He wants to avoid having to change his brochure every time his prices change.

Question 3. Show your proof

- Use testimonials from satisfied customers and other third-party references to confirm and support your stated benefits.
- These should be as numerous and as precise as possible. You can never have too many testimonials.

Question 4. How you reduce the risk

- Explain the details of your guarantee.
- Explain exactly how a customer can avail himself of it.
- Explain any procedures you have for handling complaints.

Example

Boris prints his guarantee in full on the back page of his brochure.

Question 5. What the customer should do next

- Strongly recommend that the customer *acts* by contacting your company as soon as possible and entirely without obligation.
- Always include an order form in your brochure. This should allow the reader either to place an order and pay for it or to request that you contact him to discuss his requirements.
- Explain exactly how he will benefit by responding immediately (for example, offer an introductory discount or free gift or something free that enhances your business image at the same time).

Example

Boris offers a free, eight-page guide entitled 'The Ten Biggest Mistakes Made by Most DIY Experts' to any customer who requests a quotation for building work after reading his brochure. The guide concludes by advising most homeowners to use a professional builder to improve their homes.

What sort of sales brochure does your business need?

- If you sell to other businesses, get the best you can afford.
- If you sell only to the general public, choose a low-cost pamphlet or use a series of brightly coloured A4 sheets.

How to use your sales brochure to maximum effect

- Only send out copies of your brochure to *named individuals*. Never send it simply to 'The Managing Director'.
- Only send your brochure to companies whom you have *identified* as having a possible need for your product.
- Never use a black-and-white fax machine to transmit a colour sales brochure: it will look awful. Instead, make up a separate series of black-and-white A4 sheets, specifically for faxing.
- Ideally, each brochure should be accompanied by a covering letter: the more personalised this letter is the better.

Standardised sales letters: an effective, low-cost alternative

If you sell a range of products to a variety of different customers, then instead of lumping all your product and sales information into one general sales brochure, you may find it more effective and convenient to divide it between several standardised sales letters.

Example

Brian owns an employment agency that specialises in the recruitment of financial, engineering and computer staff. Instead of using one sales brochure that explains his overall service, Brian uses a series of sales letters, each of which explains a different facet of his service. For example, one letter (sent to financial directors) explains his skill in locating experienced commercial accountants; another letter (sent to computer managers) explains his skill in recruiting computer staff; another letter (sent to engineering/production directors) explains his skill regarding engineering staff and so on.

By these means, Brian offers a specific and relevant sales message to each employer. As he says: how will his ability to locate and recruit a first-class accountant impress someone who is looking for an experienced electronics engineer?

Finally, by replacing his sales brochure with a series of shorter sales letters, Brian has discovered other advantages.

- They are cheaper and faster to produce, and cheaper to post.
- They can be easily adapted/updated.
- They take less time to read. (Brian believes that no senior executive has the time or inclination to read more than one page of a supplier's sales document.)

Successful entrepreneurs look after their files and forms

Never underestimate the power or usefulness of files. They can often prove invaluable. In particular, make sure you maintain an accurate, up-to-date record of all your customers.

Maintain a separate customer card on each customer

This should include the following details:

- The customer's address/telephone number/fax number
- Type of business
- Names of key individuals
- Their personal data, where known (eg, birthdays, hobbies, etc)
- The best time of day to contact the customer
- The date/details of each contact with the customer
- Details and dates of any sales made, plus any complaints
- Invoice and payment details of these sales.

Sell more by paying attention to your administrative forms!

- For example, every customer who buys from you receives at least an invoice or a receipt. These pieces of paper advertise the price they have paid for their purchase. Why not allow them to say something complimentary about your business at the same time?

- Either have your sales message preprinted on to your invoices, or else have it put on to a stamp and stamp your paperwork accordingly. Choose messages like:
  - The company that guarantees everything it sells!
  - Manchester's No 1 supplier of X!
  - The company that contacts you and saves you money!
  - The company that delivers overnight at no extra cost!
- Amazingly, most small businesses send out invoices (and other forms) containing *huge blank spaces*. Imagine paying for an advert in a newspaper and then leaving it blank!

Wordprocessing your business

Wordprocessors (by which I mean either a dedicated machine, plus printer, or a personal computer, plus a wordprocessing software package, plus printer) can be fairly expensive to buy. You will not get much change from £1000. However, they can massively reduce the time you have to spend on a variety of tasks. *Check them out.*

4
Seven easy ways to sell more to your present customers

This is your third step towards sales success. Start increasing your sales by paying closer attention to those people who already know you and your product: ie, your present customers.

The basic rule: keep selling yourself and your products!

Never take your present sales or customers for granted. Always be on the lookout for new ways of improving your sales operation.

Here are seven practical suggestions for how to maintain your sales edge. None of them is foolproof but all are highly practical ways of maximising the sales potential of your present customers. Try to make them a permanent feature of *your* sales operation.

1. The 80:20 rule

According to experts, roughly 80 per cent of our sales come from roughly 20 per cent of our customers. This simplistic principle is known in the sales world as the 80:20 rule.

Rather than argue with its arithmetic, you should consider its underlying message which may be expressed thus:

- Some customers are more valuable to you than others.
- You should therefore devote a correspondingly large amount of your time and effort to satisfying and looking after these valuable customers.

Although every customer deserves good service, you should make a point of doing that bit more for those who matter most.

Examples

Bonnie runs a florist shop, not far from the city centre. Although she enjoys a reasonable amount of passing trade, the bulk of her regular business comes (in the form of telephoned orders) from half a dozen local hotels and the nearby head office of a large multinational corporation.

Bonnie has a small van and a young assistant to deliver these telephoned orders, usually within 24 hours. Regarding payment, Bonnie sends a monthly account to each of these larger customers, which is due for settlement within 30 days thereafter. Apart from permitting these customers to settle their bills over a period of time, Bonnie offers no other financial inducement to buy and – because she gets on well with most of them over the phone – she has not felt it necessary to visit any of these customers personally.

One day, she receives no orders from the multinational. What is more, three days later, her two largest hotel customers also stop ordering. Between them (as she now discovers) they account for 25 per cent of her business. Thus, rather anxiously, she telephones both of them to find out the reason for their silence.

She discovers that both have been lured away by a rival florist, operating from the city centre, who has offered them a 20 per cent price reduction plus same-day delivery plus 60 days' credit in return for guaranteed monthly minimum orders.

By not taking steps to ensure the 100 per cent satisfaction of her most valuable customers, Bonnie has violated the 80:20 rule and allowed a competitor to steal a quarter of her sales.

Hilary is the bedroom and soft furnishings buyer for a major UK chain-store. She buys duvet covers and matching pillow slips from three different sources. From two large manufacturers she buys a wide range of medium-priced standard designs, while from a small company – owned by *Clyde* – she sources a smaller, more expensive range of individual designs. The products of all three suppliers sell equally well and seem to satisfy most of the store's customers.

One day, Hilary and the rest of her colleagues in the buying department receive a circular from the store's finance director. It instructs them to reduce the number of their suppliers by applying the following rule: unless the supplier is a special case, no further purchases are to be made from any company who has not been assessed for quality by the store's inspectors.

Fortunately, because the chain-store is one of his major customers, Clyde has been assiduously observing the 80:20 rule. Each week, for example, he makes a point of visiting one of the store's branches in order to talk to staff and handle any queries. Then, each month, he visits the store's head office and sees Hilary to discuss how his products are performing. On top of this, every six months or so, he invites Hilary and another colleague to visit his factory unit in the provinces to see the design process in action. Lastly, every Christmas, he makes sure to send Hilary (and at least four managers at the store's larger branches) a brand new duvet cover and pillow slip.

As a result of this careful attention, as soon as Hilary receives the circular she telephones Clyde to explain the situation. Between them, they agree on the following: first, in the short term, Hilary will make Clyde's company a 'special case' to whom the circular need not apply; second, she will arrange for the store's quality inspectors to visit Clyde's company in about three months' time, and will brief him on what to expect when they call. In short, unlike Bonnie, Clyde need not worry about losing business.

2. The 'wooing' sales technique

Customers who are serious about buying rarely place major importance on price. In their minds, other factors such as suitability, reliability and convenience are much more important. This is why most professional salespeople are trained to sell their products on the basis of their benefits and to save all mention of price until all other factors have been dealt with.

By contrast, entrepreneurs who lack this sales training and knowledge frequently make the mistake of assuming that price is all-important. As a result, they rarely obtain the best price for their product or service, especially from regular customers to whom they frequently give unnecessarily large discounts.

Start wooing your regular customers: do not depend on price

To appreciate this piece of advice, think of one of your regular customers who buys from you at a generous discount. Then ask yourself this question:

What is the major reason why this customer buys from me?

If the major reason *is* price, you have a problem. Why? Because it means that as soon as a cheaper or cut-price supplier appears on the scene, bang goes your precious customer!

The way to tackle this problem is to try to start putting across to this difficult customer *all the other benefits he receives from dealing with you*.

For example, apart from (obviously!) giving all his needs and orders the most-favoured treatment, try the following:

- Send him a personal letter explaining how important customer satisfaction is to you and your business. Include a list of all the benefits he (and other customers) receive from dealing with you. End by reminding him to let you know, as soon as possible, if he experiences any problems with your service or if there is anything else you can do for him.
- Make a point of doing this regularly: for example, once every six weeks. Not only is a letter a more cost-effective method of maintaining contact than (say) arranging a personal appointment, it is usually also more formal and more effective than telephoning. This is because the written word always carries more weight than the spoken word.
- Vary the contents of your letters. For example, keep the customer up to date with the latest news of your business. Mention any new contracts you have won or include details of testimonials from other satisfied customers.
- In addition, maintain your other regular methods of contact (telephone/appointment) as usual.
- In short, woo this regular customer just as you would a new customer who has yet to buy from you.

Choose your moment and reduce your discount

After you have wooed your customer for a while, you must choose your moment to strike. It may be at New Year; it may be on the occasion of a new order/series of orders placed by the customer; it may be any time that you consider appropriate, although ideally it should be at a personal meeting. Whatever the moment, this is what you may say:

- Remind the customer of your mutual association over the past few months/years.

- Remind him of the *good service and other benefits* he has received from you. If necessary, draw his attention to the additional specific concessions that he receives, that are not offered to other customers.

- Explain that, in order to *maintain this level of service*, you are obliged to raise the price he pays for the products he receives.

- Lastly, be prepared to justify your proposed increase by reference to your standard prices or to those enjoyed by lesser customers. Very often, a customer's main price concern is simply to maintain his position in the discount pecking order.

- *Note*. An obvious alternative to raising your prices is to get the customer to raise his level of orders. However, to avoid giving away something for nothing, you should (if possible) arrange to back-date the appropriate discount in accordance with the quantities actually ordered. For example, if in order to receive an additional 15 per cent discount, customer X agrees to buy 100 units per month, you should charge him at the *standard* rate for all goods supplied and then issue him a three-monthly credit note for the agreed discount, *provided he has ordered 300 units over the relevant three months.*

- Naturally – even after all this – your customer may remain adamant that he will either buy from you at his present (heavily discounted) prices or not at all. You must prepare for this eventuality accordingly. You must know exactly what profit the customer brings you and how important that sum is to your business. Once you have found out these financial details you can then decide whether to continue dealing with the customer on his terms, or walk away.

Generally speaking, an entrepreneur's biggest obstacle in sorting out these problems of overgenerous or historical discounts is his own fear that, without this price concession, he has nothing else left to attract the customer. As you can see, this is a psychological rather than a commercial constraint.

3. The 'homo sapiens' sales technique

This technique is especially useful when you are selling to other companies. The bigger the company, the better this technique works. It is based upon the simple fact that inside every buyer lurks a human being. It may be expressed thus:

Regard every customer as a human being first, buyer second.

More specifically, the homo sapiens sales technique is concerned with how you exploit the innate humanity of your typical customer in order to stay ahead of your competitors.

Examples

Clementine owns a small company that manufactures cork notice-boards. Although she sells a few by mail order, most of her sales are to other companies throughout Europe and the UK (for example, large and medium-sized chain-stores, stationery and office equipment suppliers, high-street stationers, gift shops, catalogue companies, etc). Of these, her biggest customers by far are the chain-stores, numbering about 40.

Ever since starting her business, Clementine has been a firm believer in the homo sapiens sales technique. This is how she applies it:

- Whenever she meets or speaks with a major customer, she devotes a certain amount of time to getting to know him as a person (she enquires about his family, interests, star sign, favourite pastimes, etc).
- Afterwards, she jots down these personal details and enters them in the customer's file.
- She repeats this process at every opportunity until she gradually builds up a picture of the individual concerned.
- She does the same for his assistant and/or secretary.
- By acquiring this information, Clementine is in a position to promote herself and her company actively, as follows:
  - Whenever Clementine meets a particular customer she is able to interest and entertain him far better through knowing his likes and dislikes. She thus avoids being just another sales appointment in the eyes of the customer.
  - Every birthday and Christmas, each customer receives a card (promoting the name of Clementine's company) together with a personalised gift. For example, if a buyer likes opera, he receives two opera tickets; if he likes fish, he receives some smoked salmon; if he just likes work but his wife likes art, he receives two tickets to a new painting exhibition, and so on.

Her Christmas offerings are therefore much more welcome than those of other suppliers.

- Periodically, each customer receives a written update of Clementine's company (new orders gained, awards won, change of address, etc), together with a small, personalised gift. Inevitably, each customer learns to associate her company with tasteful (albeit small) gifts, and reciprocates accordingly.
- Because Clementine also looks after the customer's assistant/secretary, she rarely experiences difficulty in getting through to the customer himself – unlike some of her competitors.
- The strength of her relations with her customers also allows Clementine to sidestep other typical problems that can affect small suppliers to large companies. For example, if the customer's company delays payment of an invoice, Clementine can usually quickly discover the reason for the delay and act accordingly.

Alternatively, in cases where her customer (ie, buyer) is required to exercise his *discretion* (to prune the number of suppliers used or to impose general conditions of payment or supply) Clementine is usually treated more leniently than other suppliers.

Penelope owns a small dog-grooming business. Whenever a customer brings her a dog to be groomed or clipped, Penelope always takes its name, age and birthday as well as the name and address of its owner. Then, each Christmas and birthday, she sends the dog a card together with a reminder of her grooming services. This amusing personal service plays a major part in helping Penelope to build up her customer loyalty and to stand out from her competitors.

4. The 'Christmas tree' sales technique

For four short weeks every year, Christmas tree entrepreneurs appear on forecourts and street corners throughout the country and sell millions of trees. It is a wonderful example of how to exploit customer demand and offers an important lesson to entrepreneurs everywhere. Hence the sales technique named after it, which may be phrased as follows:

- Identify in advance a specific customer need which you do not usually cater for.

- Acquire the necessary resources to cater for this need, add it to the range of products/services that you usually offer and inform the customer accordingly.

As with most sales techniques, the trick is to adapt the principle involved to your particular business.

Examples

Rupert owns a high-street printing business that offers a range of printing services to companies and individuals alike.

Every two months, to increase sales, Rupert buys and displays a different product which he feels is likely to appeal to his customers. Over the past year, such products have included:

- a range of mid-price pens;
- a range of different sized cork noticeboards;
- a range of multipurpose stamps with messages like: Read Before Destroying, I Love You, Note My Change Of Address, In Emergencies, Please Phone;
- a range of personal horoscope stationery, each containing a paragraph of highly complimentary astrological data on the star sign in question;
- a range of small, multi-use, low-priced stickers (100 per pack) with messages like: Hand-Made, Please Do Not Touch, Back In Five Minutes, Fragile, Out Of Order, Only 99p, No Smoking, Hello Sexy.

Buzz is a self-employed electrician. Like Rupert, he too has given careful thought to the additional needs of his customers, with a view to satisfying them and thus boosting his income.

Buzz's chosen method is this: before leaving any domestic customer for whom he has just completed an electrical repair or installation, he explains that he has just started selling a range of reliable but inexpensive electrical items that might make life a little easier and safer for his customers.

Such items (all described and listed on a leaflet which Buzz gives to the customer) include: rubber-handled screwdrivers, adaptors, timer-plugs, small humidifiers (to reduce damp), fuses, batteries, car battery jump-leads, door and window alarms, personal safety bleepers and so on.

Having discovered a supplier who offers him an excellent discount and 48-hour delivery, Buzz need only carry a small stock of these products in his van.

Generally speaking, he sells something to most customers and, although sales are steady rather than spectacular, his weekly income has increased by an average of 10 per cent. He intends to develop this extra sales service further by leafleting local housing estates with details of his products as well as his service as an electrician. If nothing else, he feels that his extra service will give him an edge over his competitors.

5. The 'mother-in-law' sales technique

This sales technique derives from a famous sales story.

A young salesman, on his first day with Irving & Irving (Hardware and Sports Equipment Retailers), is told to keep an eye on *Harry* (the store's top salesman) to see how customers should be handled. Within minutes, he sees a customer walk into the shop and bump into Harry. The next quarter of an hour holds him spellbound.

First, he sees the customer buy a small, inexpensive cake-stand. Next, after a moment or two of laughter, he sees Harry offering the customer a fishing rod, then, a pair of waders, followed by a net, six packets of hooks, four artificial baits, a waterproof jacket and, finally, a large umbrella. The customer duly settles the bill of nearly £200 and happily leaves the store clutching his purchases. Impressed with his mentor's sales efforts, the youngster asks him how on earth he did it.

'It was no trouble really,' explains Harry. 'The customer asked for a cake-stand: I asked why, and he said his wife needed it because her mother was coming to stay for the weekend. I could tell he was a bit bothered by the idea of entertaining his mother-in-law all weekend, so I suggested to him – why not go fishing?'

The moral is: sometimes customers are perfectly willing to consider buying more, but they need *prompting*. They need you to take the initiative and make appropriate suggestions.

In such cases, your first step is to probe for additional customer needs. The basis for Harry's inspired suggestion to his customer (to go fishing) was his discovery of the arrival of the mother-in-law: a discovery only made by asking the customer *why* he wanted the cake-stand in the first place.

Adapt this technique to your own business

- You own a newsagents. A man walks in and buys a Valentine card.

  Why not point to a nearby cluster of gift-wrapped chocolates and ask if he has considered adding chocolates to his gift of a card?

- You own another newsagents. A local walks in and buys a packet of cigarettes.

  Why not hand him a leaflet with details of all the magazines you supply and ask him to show it to the family at home?

- You own a hotel with one or two video games machines.

  Why not give each arriving guest (or their children) a free token for these machines? You are sure to increase guest-spending as a result.

  Or why not hand each departing guest a leaflet promoting your special offers that apply to any further overnight or weekend stays within the next (say) eight weeks?

- You are a self-employed driving instructor.

  Whenever someone enquires about lessons, why not ask if they have any other family members who might require lessons?

- You own a laundrette.

  Why not hand each departing customer a leaflet explaining your service washes?

6. The 'frog' sales technique

Frogs do not sell products. Neither, so far as we know, do they run their own businesses. However, they do feed and their feeding technique is particularly instructive for anyone who wishes to master the art of selling.

The frog technique, used both for feeding and selling, is simply this: keep your eyes wide open and your tongue at the ready! Specifically, keep your eyes open for any additional sales opportunities when you visit customers.

Examples

Bernie is a self-employed painter and decorator. One evening, he visits a house to quote for the job of repainting a kitchen. His quote is accepted on the spot and he returns the following day to do the job. By 6pm he has finished and, after receiving the approval of his customer, Bernie is paid and bids his farewell. Bernie has never heard of the frog sales technique.

Pablo is a self-employed painter and decorator who *does* know the frog technique. When he visits a house to quote for a similar kitchen job, he behaves quite differently from Bernie. First, when he arrives at the house, he keeps his *eyes open*. For example, he notes down any visible defects in the exterior paintwork. He also quickly inspects the windows and porch. Only then does he ask the owner about the kitchen job and furnish an appropriate quote.

Next, if at all possible, he has a quick look at the interior paintwork to see what else might require decorating. Finally, judging his moment, he mentions one or two of the defects he has seen around the house and asks whether the owner would like him to sort them out, as well as the kitchen.

As it happens, the owner accepts Pablo's kitchen quote but declines his offer to tackle the other jobs. However, when Pablo returns to do the job two days later, the owner tells him that he would like him to do these extra jobs after all.

7. The 'SAS' sales technique

SAS stands for Sell After Selling. The technique is this: always stay in touch with your customers. Not only are they the best advertisement for your product/service, but they are also likely to buy more – provided you ask.

Examples

Joshua owns a small garage and car repair service. In order to maximise the sales potential of his customers, Joshua has designed a customer work form on which he meticulously records details of:

- all product sales/repair work performed;
- name/address/telephone number of the customer;
- details (where possible) of the customer's car, including age/make/road-tax expiry date/MOT expiry date, etc.

He uses this information to increase his sales, as follows:

- Every three months, each customer receives a leaflet through the post reminding him of Joshua's service and mechanical expertise. For example, his latest leaflet, sent out to all customers on

1 November, carried the headline: 'Having problems with *your* car in the cold? Relax: simply telephone Joshua on....'

By contrast, previous leaflets have promoted Joshua's fast repair service, his range of spare parts and his MOT service. In all his leaflets, Joshua stresses his personal and friendly approach. His constant message is:

'If you have a problem with *your* car, come to me first.'

- Each customer who spends more than, say, £100 on a repair or on a new part receives a telephone call from Joshua, the following week, to enquire how the new part or repair is performing. Joshua invariably finds that the customer is both surprised by and grateful for this personal attention.
- Each customer for whom Joshua does any MOT work receives an annual note reminding him to renew his MOT. This frequently leads to the customer returning his car for a check-up.
- Each customer receives an annual note reminding him to renew his road tax. This note also includes details of Joshua's sales and repair service.
- By staying in touch and by paying such attention to his customers, Joshua has no trouble in obtaining referrals or testimonials. His leaflets promote and publicise these glowing references accordingly.

Karina owns a house-cleaning business. Her clients are evenly divided between estate agents – acting on behalf of landlords or absent owners – and individual houseowners. Karina applies the SAS sales technique as follows:

- After every job, she presents the client with a standard form which she calls a customer satisfaction form. This form permits the client to indicate his level of approval for how well the property was cleaned, how responsive Karina's company was to his needs, what value for money the company offered, and so on.
- Karina then uses this customer satisfaction form in two ways:
  - Any negative comments are carefully heeded and used as a basis for improving her service. Where improvements are made, as a result of such comments, they are immediately communicated to the client so as to reassure him that the cause of his displeasure has been eliminated. Karina has found that most

clients are both surprised and impressed with this reaction to their complaints, and are happy to continue placing business with her.

- Any positive comments are used (with client approval) in her verbal sales presentation to other clients and are incorporated into her sales brochure.

● Karina regularly maintains contact with all her previous customers to increase her chances of obtaining repeat business. Corporate customers are telephoned weekly and individuals are telephoned/written to monthly. The emphasis is always the same: her company is available at any time to cope with any cleaning or clearance job, no matter how dirty or difficult.

Loretta is an aromatherapist who massages away a variety of physical complaints with aromatic oils. Since she has only just started up in business, she depends heavily on the SAS technique.

She asks every satisfied customer whether they know of anyone who might benefit from her service. To those clients who respond positively she gives a leaflet listing her services and explaining how they help, and asks whether they would pass it on to the person in question. About one in six of these pass-ons results in a new client visiting her for treatment.

Mark owns a small hotel. He always makes a point of sending a personal letter to the home address of each departing guest, thanking them for using his hotel and expressing his hope that they will return before long.

He also asks them (if they have the time) to comment on the hotel's service and to let him know if there are any additional services they would like to enjoy on their next visit.

Finally, he encloses a voucher entitling them to, for example, a bottle of vintage French wine when they eat in the hotel's restaurant during their next stay. Mark varies these offers to meet the different preferences of his customers.

Percy is a self-employed landscape gardener. One of his biggest problems is that many potential customers are unfamiliar with exactly what he does and what good value he offers.

To overcome this ignorance, at the end of each job he asks each satisfied customer to refer him to any family members or friends who might benefit from his service. If a customer provides him with a referral, Percy notes down the name and address of the individual concerned and immediately sends the latter a personal note. Percy follows this up with a phone call to answer any queries personally and find out what needs doing.

5

Sell more by finding new customers

This is your fourth step to sales success. Learn how to find new customers.

Six easy sources of new customers for your business

1. Your own business records

Your best source of new business is anyone and everyone who contacts – or has already contacted – you with a sales enquiry. Treat *all* callers with the greatest of care and, above all, be sure to ask for their names, addresses and phone numbers.

2. Your local area

Your second best source is likely to be your local area. Look around you; think about who may have a use for your product and work out a way of reaching them.

3. Your main local library

Libraries are excellent sources of potential customers. Have a close look at the following reference publications:

The Retail Directory (Newman) lists all UK department and chainstores, plus their respective buyers. Absolutely essential if you want to sell to the retail trade or if you need to know who buys electrical products for Boots Plc, for example.

Kompass lists all the larger UK companies. There is also a European *Kompass*. Ideal if you want to know which products are made by what company, where.

Stubbs Buyer's Guide (Dunn & Bradstreet) lists all the larger UK companies. Ideal if you are selling to businesses.

Municipal Yearbook is a comprehensive guide to the services and key personnel within the public sector. An essential reference for anyone selling to local authorities.

Yellow Pages. Most main libraries carry a complete set.

Local company registers. Many main libraries operate and maintain a local company register, usually on microfiche or computer. Ask your librarian for details.

BRAD Directory (Newspapers and Magazines) lists all UK national and provincial newspapers, plus all consumer and trade magazines. Includes circulation data, advertising and subscription costs and key personnel on each publication. Ideal reference guide to all UK publications.

4. The Yellow Pages *database*

Yellow Pages will supply you with any list of UK companies (for example, craft shops or computer software companies) and, if required, for any postal code district. Contact: Business Database, Database House, 8 Waterside Drive, Langley, Slough, Berkshire SL3 6EZ; telephone 0753 583311.

5. Specialist company-list suppliers

From these companies (usually called list brokers) you can buy a list of just about any type of company. However, before doing so, check on three things: when was the list compiled, how was it compiled and does it include telephone numbers?

For further information, contact: Direct Marketing Association UK, Haymarket House, Oxendon Street, London SW1Y 4EE; telephone 071 321 2525.

6. Magazines

Consumer magazines often contain useful business leads. For example, their advertisements sometimes contain up-to-date lists of retailers and other stockists, together with all-important phone numbers.

Trade magazines are usually available on free subscription and frequently contain useful information. In addition, many trade magazines have their own Yearbook containing lists of buyers and suppliers for the trade. Consult the *BRAD Directory* (see above) for details.

How entrepreneurs find new customers in practice

Clint is a self-employed painter and decorator. For the past five years he has barely scraped a living. As a one-man band, his biggest problem is finding new jobs while working on those he already has. After a full day's work he usually spends most evenings pricing and quoting for new jobs – nearly always against fierce competition. One day, he decides that instead of waiting for new customers to contact him, he is going to contact them first!

He therefore spends a few weekends driving around the local estates and suburbs, looking for houses in need of exterior decoration. Armed with a set of *standard quotation forms* in his glove compartment, he prices these jobs on the spot and pops the quotation through the letter-box.

Finally, to make it as easy as possible for the customer to respond, Clint makes two additions:

- He includes a self-addressed reply-paid postcard with his quotation, for those customers who prefer to reply by post.
- On the back of each card is a prominent testimonial from a satisfied customer, plus three boxes for the customer to tick, as follows:

  ☐ I am absolutely delighted with your quote. Please telephone me on ... to arrange a convenient starting date. Signed ....

  ☐ I would like to take advantage of your low-price quotation within the next three months. Please telephone me some time over the next few weeks on ... to arrange details. Signed ....

  ☐ Unfortunately, I cannot take advantage of your attractive quotation. However, I would like you to telephone me some time next week on ... to arrange to give me a separate quotation for .... Signed ....

Digger is a self-employed builder-cum-renovator. Since he lives in a university town with a large number of student-occupied flats, he has targeted landlords as a source of new business. To begin with, he makes a point of knowing exactly when each of the three university terms begins and ends. Then, one week before the beginning of each term, he telephones the university office responsible for student accommodation and requests a list of landlords whom he may approach for a flat.

Armed with this list of potential customers, Digger waits until about a fortnight before the end of each term and then telephones each landlord on his list to find out if he requires any renovations or repairs done over the university vacation, ie while most of the student flats are unoccupied.

Whatever work he is given over the vacation, Digger makes sure to recontact each landlord just before the new term starts to remind them of his service and to enquire whether they are likely to need any maintenance work done, during term time.

Even though Digger rarely comes across a landlord who offers him work immediately, his persistence in maintaining contact not only helps him to get to know a wide variety of new customers, but it nearly always results in new work.

Abraham is a self-employed electrician. He has a different method of finding new customers. Each Friday morning, from 8.30am to 11.30am, Abraham telephones companies throughout his local city to find out the name of the executive who supervises their electrical repair and maintenance work (anything from mending fuses to reorganising underfloor cables).

Once he has acquired the name of this supervisor, he tries to have a quick word with him to find out whether he employs a regular firm of electricians for his emergency/routine electrical work, or whether he simply rings a firm at random when the need arises.

Whatever his reply, Abraham tries to get an appointment to see him. This is because Abraham believes that personal contact always helps him to sell his service as an electrician. He therefore takes every opportunity to meet potential customers face to face.

Like Digger, Abraham does not often come across a company which needs his services there and then. It is only through regular telephone contact, and occasional personal contact, that he becomes known and then engaged. Nevertheless, new contracts are now beginning to come his way on a regular basis.

One of Abraham's best qualities is his refusal to give up. He is always on the lookout for sales opportunities. For example, sometimes he encounters a company that occupies part of a large tower block. Usually, in such a case, the company's maintenance requirements are already catered for by a main contractor who oversees the entire building. In this situation, instead of just letting the matter drop, Abraham normally asks for the name of the electrical supervisor at the main contractor and promptly telephones him to offer his services as a subcontractor.

Another interesting thing about Abraham is his determination to get ahead of his competitors. Thus, recently, he has become a member of his local Chamber of Commerce. This membership not only provides him with a number of useful introductions at its various functions, but it also gives him and his business an extra edge of respectability over his competitors.

Rajiv is a self-employed plumber and general handyman. At the moment, he uses two different methods of finding new business.

First, he regularly telephones a number of local estate agents both to introduce himself and his skills and to sell them the idea of recommending his plumbing service to their clients. If, for example, they know of any vendors or purchasers who need a central heating system installed or serviced, then why not recommend him and receive a commission for their trouble?

In addition, to those agents who manage rented property he sells the idea of using him to cope with any plumbing problems, or any general maintenance or repairs. By having a reliable plumber and repair-man on hand (he says), they can offer hassle-free tenancies to both their houseowners and their tenants.

Rajiv's second method of finding new customers is to contact local suppliers of washing machines/tumble dryers, etc to get them to recommend his plumbing and installation service to their customers.

This approach has proved very successful with several suppliers who now use Rajiv exclusively for all their installations – not least because Rajiv is always available on Saturdays.

Naturally, whenever he installs a washing machine for one of the suppliers' customers, Rajiv always leaves him with his business card and a reminder to call if ever he needs a plumber in a hurry.

Although neither of Rajiv's methods of attracting new customers is especially clever or original, they do bring in extra business and, equally important, they are helping him to build up a network of useful commercial contacts across two different trades. For the future, Rajiv is currently researching names and addresses for a telephone campaign to all local housing associations to see whether he can secure himself a long-term contract to maintain some of their properties. After that, he plans a similar campaign aimed at retirement homes and then restaurants.

Daisy owns a hairdresser's. Her chosen method of finding new business is to team up with Poppy, the owner of a nearby beauty salon. Every week, Daisy passes details of all her customers to Poppy and vice versa. By swopping information in this way, each of them is able to build up a list of potential new customers for their own particular service.

Daisy uses her list as the basis for a bi-monthly mailshot that publicises her full range of hair treatments and offers a 15 per cent introductory discount to all first-time customers.

Olga owns a health-food shop called Body Temple that sells wholefoods, health products and aromatic oils.

As part of her ongoing effort to find new customers, Olga has developed contacts among all the major environmentalist organisations and regularly attends their local fêtes and other functions.

Whenever possible, she hires a stall and actively publicises Body Temple's location and products. To those people who come from outside the area, she explains and promotes her 48-hour mail-order service. Furthermore, to encourage people to leave their names and addresses, she usually holds a free raffle and offers a small prize to the winner. (For similar ideas see also page 48.)

Her aim is gradually to build up a significant database of health-conscious customers through which to market and sell her products on a regular basis.

In addition to maintaining contact with environmentalists, Olga also gives regular health-food demonstrations and tastings to meetings of the Women's Institute, social meetings of the Liberal Democrats and numerous other groups.

Lastly, she keeps in touch with the student officials at the local university and regularly publicises her special offers to students on posters throughout the campus.

Cathy owns Wuthering Heights – a 15-bedroom hotel in south Yorkshire. Her approach to finding new business is to sell herself to local companies. Every week, she sets aside enough time to ring at least 40 companies, to introduce them to the services she offers and to explain how they can make use of them.

When calling, if she cannot speak directly to the company's managing director, she speaks to his secretary or PA. She then follows up each telephone conversation with a personalised letter and a copy of her 'Business Services' leaflet. This leaflet promotes the convenient location of the hotel and explains the various facilities on offer to companies. Its basic message is simple: whatever a company needs, whether it is a sales meeting, a PR presentation, entertainment of foreign buyers, or simply a staff party, Wuthering Heights can help.

Having promoted herself in this way for nearly two years, Cathy has built up a sizeable network of contacts among the local business community and is now looking to extend the hotel and expand her services even further.

Violet is a self-employed landscape gardener in Nottingham. A year ago, she nearly went bankrupt through lack of business. Fortunately, she just managed to save herself in time. This is how she did it.

First, she told herself that her business problems were only temporary, that she was definitely going to succeed – the only question was how!

Second, she thought long and hard about the gardening service she offered and why so few people were buying it. Eventually, she decided that she needed to offer something more specific. She therefore came up with the idea of offering a herb garden service. She would offer to design and plant a range of three different sized herb gardens (small, medium or large) for an all-in price to include a four-week maintenance programme.

To this end, she designed an attractive yellow leaflet to promote her expertise in designing and planting herb gardens and to highlight the nutritional powers of the herbs involved. Having established her new service, Violet then set about selling it. Her aim was to broadcast it as fast and as cheaply as possible to the maximum number of potential customers. She decided on a leaflet drop.

The following weekend, therefore, she recruited half a dozen smart young people, armed each of them with a sackful of brightly coloured leaflets and ferried them to various affluent suburbs throughout the city. In all, 2000 leaflets were pushed through the letter-boxes of 2000 potential customers, within 24 hours. The next weekend, Violet repeated the process in different parts of the city and, the weekend after that, in several outlying towns.

The results of this leafleting exceeded all Violet's expectations. Her business recovered and is now thriving. A perfect illustration of how to sell your way out of trouble.

Myrtle has her own small picture-framing business. Two years ago, fed up with receiving only a handful of replies to her advertisements, Myrtle plucked up the courage to go out and look for business herself.

She spent three months visiting every shop she could find that sold any sort of pictures, posters or photographs. To each shopowner or manager she proposed that she handle all their customers' framing requirements in return for giving the shop a share of the price charged. She also offered the shop a small, attractive counter-sign announcing: 'Ask about our fast, efficient framing service!'

At the end of the three months, over 20 shops carried her sign and Myrtle's order-book was already growing.

She then set about exploiting her newly established shop network by writing to other shops, slightly further afield, with details of her 'Retail Framing Service' and enclosing a couple of testimonials from owners of shops whose customers had already benefited from her expertise. By this means, she added a further eight shops to her network.

Now Myrtle no longer has to rely upon advertisements. She has all the framing business she can handle.

Rita owns a smallish, city-centre café/restaurant. Competition is fierce so, rather than sit behind the counter forlornly waiting for customers to come to her, Rita makes a point of taking her food service to the customer.

Every day, at 10.30am and 4.00pm, she visits each of the six office blocks in the vicinity with a large basket of homemade sandwiches, cakes and pies. In addition, at 1pm, she sends an assistant on a similar trip to service those customers who are unable to leave the office during lunchtime. As a result of these efforts, Rita sometimes sells more to customers whom she visits than to those who visit her. Two doors down, one of her competitors is still gazing at empty tables!

Sebastian owns a sports shop in a small northern town. To boost his sales during the months of October and November, he holds a series of weekly demonstrations of his fluorescent safety wear for pedestrians and cyclists at schools throughout the area. By doing this, not only does Sebastian sell more safety wear, he also has an opportunity to hand out leaflets on his other new products in the run up to Christmas.

Adrian, aged 21, has recently started his own business selling novelty egg-timers that he makes himself in his garage. As it happened, initial sales trials in local shops went so well that he decided to try selling them further afield.

Accordingly, he visited his local reference library, skimmed through the latest copy of *The Retail Directory* and jotted down the names and telephone numbers of the relevant buyers in all the major UK chain-stores. The following week, he telephoned each buyer to introduce himself and to find out what he had to do to get them to buy his egg-timers.

After noting and duly complying with the respective procedures of each buyer, Adrian was rewarded with two reasonably large orders for his product and several other promises of orders in the near future.

At present, he is compiling a list of European buyers, from the European edition of *Kompass*, to whom he intends to write with a sample of his egg-timers. His overall aim is to establish a base of 100 large buyers who know him and his product, so as to take advantage of next Christmas's peak buying period.

6

Sell more by mastering the technique of telephone selling

This is your fifth step to sales success. Learn how to use the phone like an expert. Although this chapter is mainly for the benefit of entrepreneurs who sell to other businesses, it contains a number of tips that apply to all types of telephone sales.

In practice, selling over the phone to new customers usually requires at least two phone calls:

- A canvassing call
- A follow-up sales call.

In addition, because many customers take time to make up their minds, a third (or fourth) call is often needed to close the sale and secure the order.

Your canvassing call

Before picking up the phone, be prepared

Speaking to complete strangers under time pressure requires preparation. Therefore, before picking up the phone to a new customer, you must have something to say and something to send them. You should also have some ready means of recording their details and comments. This applies to all sales calls made over the phone.

For example, make sure you have the following:

- A sales script: ie, a list of points to be made or technical data to be cited.
- A sales brochure/leaflet/letter to post or fax to the customer when you have finished speaking to him.

- A boxed set of blank record cards, with A–Z dividers, to act as your customer cards.

The aims of your canvassing call

- To introduce yourself and your product.
- To find out something about the individual needs of the buyer.
- To arrange, if necessary, to send the buyer some written information or a product sample.
- To arrange a time to call back.

Tips on what to do

Speak slowly

Nearly everyone who receives a call from a complete stranger needs at least ten seconds to adjust to what is being said. Do not therefore give out any important information (for example, your name or your company name) during this time: your listener will only be confused. Instead, start your conversation with a piece of slowly spoken waffle. This will allow your listener to 'wake up' to your strange voice.

Do not say:	Hello, it's Jane Brown from Fit For Business Limited.
Say:	Hello, Mr Buyer, I don't think that we have actually spoken together before. My name is Jane Brown. I run a company called Company Aerobics Limited that offers aerobic classes to company employees.
Or, say:	Hello, is that Mr Buyer?
	Yes.
	Hello, Mr Buyer, I don't think that we have actually spoken together before ... etc.

Speak clearly

This may sound too obvious to mention, but ask yourself this: how many times have you received a call from someone who mumbled into the phone or who used slang or who was difficult to understand. Also, make a point of holding the phone properly and speaking into the mouthpiece, not across it.

Warm up first

Before starting their live radio shows, many disc jockeys do a series of vocal exercises to warm up their vocal chords. Ideally, you should do the same before starting your tele-sales calls. Spend five minutes talk-ing, humming or singing to yourself. It may sound a bit nutty but believe me, it helps!

Most buyers are protected by a two-tier screening process

Most company buyers are either directors or senior managers. In keeping with this status, they are usually protected against interrup-tions (ie, unsolicited phone calls) by a two-tier screen. The first tier is usually the company receptionist, who is often under instructions not to accept any unsolicited sales calls – full stop. The second tier is the buyer's own secretary who is usually given more discretion as to whether or not to disturb her boss with an unsolicited call, but who nevertheless can prove equally impenetrable.

Two examples of the screening process in operation

Imagine you own a small company that sells business stationery. This is how you can be fobbed off, if you are not careful.

You: Hello, may I speak to the person who normally buys your office stationery?

Rec: Just a moment. (The receptionist now seeks advice on what to do with you.) Sorry, I'm told we're not buying any sta-tionery at the moment. Thanks for calling, goodbye.

Alternatively:

You: Hello, can you give me the name of the person who normally buys your office stationery?

Rec: Who's calling?

You: Joe Brown, from Brown's Stationery.

Rec: Just a moment. (The receptionist checks, as above.) I've just had a word with our managing director and he says to tell you that we won't need any stationery for several months, thank you. Goodbye.

How to get past reception

In most cases, all you need to do to get past the receptionist is to ask for your buyer *by name*. It is usually assumed that, if you know the buyer's name, you are familiar to him and not likely to be a nuisance or interruption. This is especially so if you give the buyer's *first name* as well as his surname.

If you do not know the buyer's name, you must persuade the receptionist to give it to you. This may be harder than you think, since receptionists are sometimes told not to part with this sort of information. The best method of obtaining the buyer's name is to try something like this:

You: I wonder if you can help me. I'd like to *send some information* to the person in charge of x (or buying x), but I don't have his name to hand. Can you tell me who that would be, please?

Note: If at this stage, the receptionist seeks advice on what to do with you, she will say that she has a caller who wants to *send information* to the buyer – not a caller who wants to *speak* to the buyer. As a result, because you are not likely to be seen as a nuisance, you will almost certainly be given the buyer's name.

If the receptionist gives you the buyer's surname, ask whether she knows his first name as well.

Once you have the buyer's name, simply ring back in about half an hour and say something like:

You: Hello, John Smith please.

Note: Never ask a receptionist whether you can speak to a buyer or whether a buyer is in or available. Simply ask for him by name and leave it at that. If you make it sound as though it is none of her business, she is unlikely to question you any further and will usually put you straight through to the buyer's office.

How to get past the buyer's secretary

When you are put through to the buyer's office you will usually be answered by the buyer's secretary. Never make the mistake of underrating the secretary. In all likelihood she has the complete confidence of her boss either to put callers through to him or to give them the diplomatic brush-off, as she sees fit.

This brush-off treatment is generally meted out to the following categories of caller:

- An unfriendly or aggressive caller.
- A caller who sounds unprofessional or dull.
- A caller who is unable to give a coherent explanation for why he wants to speak to the buyer in question.
- A new caller who sounds as though he is likely to take up a lot of the buyer's time.

The moral? Make sure, when you speak to a buyer's secretary, that you do not fall into any of the above categories!

Example

Imagine you own a small company that sells house plants, etc. You are phoning a new client company for the first time. After finding out the buyer's name (see above), you manage to get past reception and are put through to the managing director's office. This is what you should do.

Sec: Hello, Mr Smith's office.
You: Hello, is John Smith there, please?

(It is all right to ask a secretary whether her MD is available: it sounds friendlier.)

Sec: Who's calling, please?
You: Jane Brown.

(Only give your name: nothing else. The secretary may simply put you through without asking for more details.)

Sec: From which company? (Oh dear. No such luck.)
You: Brown's Office Greenery.

(Again, avoid going into any further detail.)

Sec: Can I ask what it is in connection with?

(The secretary is thorough. You must now quickly and clearly explain the reason for your call and, at the same time, reassure the secretary that you will not take up much of the MD's time.)

You: Certainly. I just need a very quick word with Mr Smith to give him one or two details about our plants and flower service and ask him a couple of questions about the sort of plants he normally buys.

Sec: Actually, to be perfectly honest, I don't think he'd be terribly interested in buying any plants.

(The secretary senses that you are only going to waste her boss's time and so begins to fob you off. You must work fast to reassure her to the contrary.)

You: Don't worry, I quite understand. Until they actually see the sort of plants we supply, most people feel the same way. That is why we normally offer a free trial first. However, to do that I just need a quick word with Mr Smith to introduce myself and to find out the sort of things he likes.

(Note how, instead of denying the likelihood of Mr Smith's lack of interest, you immediately acknowledge it as perfectly natural. This, together with your free offer, should go some way towards disarming the secretary.)

Sec: I'm awfully sorry, but he's tied up at the moment. Can I help?

(This may be the brush-off, it may not. To find out, probe.)

You: Well, since I haven't had the opportunity of speaking to Mr Smith before, I would like to introduce myself to him, when he has a free moment. Can you tell me when would be the best time to call back?

(At this point, the secretary can react in one of two ways. Either, she will suggest a good time to ring back, in which case you must thank her for her kind help and make a note to ring as requested, or she may continue to stall as follows.)

Sec: I'm sorry, but Mr Smith is a very busy man. I'm not really sure when would be a good time.

You: Look, I really don't mean to be a nuisance. I realise that Mr Smith is very busy but I'm sure he has a couple of spare minutes some time this week to have a word with me. I'd be very grateful if you would fit me into his schedule somehow.

This polite but firm plea usually does the trick: the secretary normally gives you a time to call back and all ends well. If, by contrast, she continues to try to fob you off, you have three options:

- Thank her very politely for her time and say that you are going to try calling Mr Smith tomorrow – on the offchance that he will be free.
- Ask her politely who else in the company would be worth speaking to.
- Thank her very politely for her time and say that you will first write to Mr Smith and then follow it up afterwards with a personal phone call.

Your canvassing call: an outline of what to say to the buyer

This is a general outline of how you should conduct a standard canvassing call.

- Explain to the buyer, in simple language, who you are and what your company does.
- Tell him that you are really ringing to introduce yourself and that you do not want to go into any great detail about your product there and then.
- Explain that, if he does not mind, you would like to ask him one or two questions about his business, for example ....
- Use three or four questions to try to find out something about his particular needs or concerns, regarding the type of product you supply. (See Chapter 1, above.)
- Arrange to send the buyer some written details about your product and/or a sample.
- Thank the buyer for his time and the information he has given you; then arrange a convenient time (ie, day and time) to ring back to discuss the matter further.

Note. This outline is only intended as a guide and applies mainly to initial contact with fairly uninterested buyers.

Your follow-up sales call

As its name indicates, this call is made to follow up information that you have sent to your buyer.

The aims of your follow-up call

- To clarify the buyer's needs.

- To explain how your product meets those needs.
- To answer any objections raised and to push for an order.

An outline of what to say to the buyer

This is a general outline of how you should conduct a standard follow-up call.

- Reintroduce yourself to the buyer, slowly and clearly.
- Remind him that you recently sent him written information on your product. (*Note*. Do *not* ask whether he has read this information. Although he will almost certainly have seen and skimmed through it, he is likely to deny having seen it in order to be able to postpone a decision to buy.)
- Tell the buyer that you would like to go back over what he told you last time about his company. Spend a few seconds asking him again one or two of the questions from your canvassing call, then move straight on to asking him any new questions you have planned or that you can think of, to clarify his needs.
- Rephrase and repeat back to the buyer what you think his needs are. Say something such as, 'So what you are saying, Mr Buyer, is that you are always on the lookout for something new to offer your customers, provided you can be reasonably certain that it will sell. Is that right?' If you are careful, the buyer will generally agree. If for some reason he does not agree with your assessment, simply ask him to clarify what he *is* looking for.
- Tell him that your product fits the bill! Proceed to explain exactly how your product meets his declared needs, avoiding all mention of cost/price until last. (See page 12.) When doing this, be sure to support your arguments with precise facts and, whenever possible, use testimonials, references or case histories involving other satisfied customers. The buyer will always find it easier to believe a third party rather than a salesperson.
- Answer any objections with the Welcome-Probe-Test-Answer method. If the buyer appears satisfied but will not commit himself there and then, raise some objections yourself and answer them one by one.
- As soon as you can, push for the order and try to close the sale. *Never wait for the buyer to ask whether he can buy. He won't!* (For examples of this final stage, see pages 25–8.)

Tips on what to do

Find out as much as you can about the buyer's needs

As this book makes clear, one of the vital principles of selling is that you should never attempt to list the wonderful features and advantages of your product until you know what your buyer is looking for or what *he* thinks is important. If you omit this vital first step, you run a serious risk of alienating your buyer and losing the sale.

So how much do you have to know about a buyer's needs before explaining your product?

The short answer is, as much as it takes for you to feel confident that you know the buyer's *main concern* when it comes to buying your sort of product.

Where possible, pre-plan your questions

Although most buyers (ie, directors, managers) enjoy talking about themselves and their company, they are also likely to become uncomfortable with any extended process of questioning. In order to maintain a reasonably swift flow of conversation, you will find it useful to plan a few key questions in advance.

Some key questions

Imagine you are selling handmade leather photograph albums to a buyer working for a major London department store. The type of questions you should ask would include the following:

- What sort of customers does the store cater for in the main?
- What other sorts of customer does it cater for?
- What types of album are currently sold?
- How well are they selling?
- What is the most important feature that the buyer looks for in a supplier?

The answers to these five questions alone will give you a good basis to work from. In addition, if you have time, you should also ask one or two leading questions. For example, if you have just won an order to supply another major customer (for example, a Paris store) or if you have just won an award for quality (for example, from a magazine or trade organisation), you should ask something like:

- How important is a supplier's sales record to you, when considering whether to buy?
- How important is quality assurance to you, when it comes to choosing your suppliers?

By asking these questions you oblige the buyer to acknowledge a *need* for suppliers with a proven sales record or a proven record of quality. When it comes to explaining your product, you can then demonstrate how it satisfies this need by giving details of your large Parisian order or your award for quality.

Finally, if you have time, you may also ask one or two personal questions to try to draw the buyer out a little. For instance:

- How long has the buyer been in charge of buying x, y, z?
- What does he know about the way albums are made?
- Does he ever get a chance to visit suppliers?

Explanations over the phone require verbal pictures

Explaining something over the phone is quite different from explaining something face to face. For instance, when you explain face to face, you can use all manner of facial expressions and gestures to keep your listener interested, whereas over the phone, all you have is your voice. Thus, in order to maintain the interest of a listener over the phone, a different technique is required. One such technique, which I advise you to develop, is to paint verbal pictures for your listener.

How to paint a verbal picture

Imagine you and a partner run a two-man motorbike messenger/delivery service. As part of your new business drive, you telephone the MD of a Derby-based ink manufacturing company. Your approach may go something like this.

First, you ask a few questions to find out something about the company's needs. You may discover, for instance, that it has half a dozen very important customers whose printing presses must (under all circumstances) be kept supplied with ink. In addition, you may be told that the company's own vans are not always capable of responding quickly enough to the demands of these customers: especially when it comes to despatching one-kilo emergency quantities.

Having found out a bit about the company's needs, you then try to explain how your service satisfies those needs. This is when you apply your technique of painting verbal pictures to make your explanation sound interesting and relevant. Thus, instead of simply pointing out that both you and your partner have mobile phones and that you guarantee to pick up and deliver 24 hours a day, seven days a week, paint a picture for the MD at the other end of the phone.

Tell him to imagine that he is sitting at home watching a late film on TV. Suddenly, the phone rings: it is his night-shift manager calling to say that a VIP customer in Northampton has just telephoned with an urgent order for a custom-made ink.

The manager explains that, although the ink will be ready in 45 minutes, the duty van has broken down. What is he to do? Should he wake up another driver to bring in another van, or should he arrange for the ink to go out first thing tomorrow? In addition, he reveals that another VIP customer in Lincoln has just phoned, ten minutes earlier, to say that he is likely to need an extra kilo of ink before 6am.

Tell the MD that, by retaining your organisation as a back-up delivery service, all he would have to do in such a situation is to tell his manager to make *one simple phone call* to you or your partner. The problem would then be solved. The first lot of ink would be picked up within the hour and could be in Northampton an hour later. The same bike could then return, pick up the delivery for the Lincoln customer and deliver it no later than four hours after the manager's initial phone call. Result: two VIP customers are satisfied and all the regular van drivers' work schedules remain intact for the following day, with no need for disruptive overtime arrangements.

Apply this technique to your business

Apply and adapt this technique to your particular product. Practise conjuring up real-life business situations in which your product or service comes alive and clearly meets the need of the customer.

Always match the features of your product to customer needs

Following the Classic Sales Method, you should always make your product fit the specific needs of your customer. Never waste precious telephone time explaining impressive features that are unlikely to satisfy those needs. To put it another way: imagine your product is like a piece of cloth that must be tailored to fit the individual shape of the customer to whom you are speaking. In this analogy, the needs of the customer are his measurements. (See pages 18–23, for examples.)

Answering objections over the phone

Remember to observe the Welcome-Probe-Test-Answer method when faced with objections from your customer. First, *welcome* the objection to relax him; then *probe* for the extent of the objection; then *test* it to confirm that it represents a real (not a fake) objection; finally, *answer it* with a specific and relevant rebuttal, ideally prepared in advance.

Each stage of this process is important, but none more so than the first, when you welcome what the customer has to say. When selling over the phone it is especially important to allow the customer to feel relaxed about his particular views, even if you then proceed to rebut each and every one of them! If you fail to relax him, you run a serious risk of the call being terminated before you even have a chance to overcome his worries.

Objections and the iceberg rule

Objections are like icebergs: they can often remain hidden from view. This is especially true over the phone when the customer himself is no more than a voice.

Thus, for example, after impressing a buyer with your product, you call back the following morning to close the sale and discover to your horror that the same customer has decided not to buy after all. What went wrong? The answer is: you failed to observe the *iceberg rule.*

The iceberg rule amounts to this: an objection raised by a customer may only be the tip of his concern. Thus, in order to convince someone to buy, you must answer *all* his possible objections. And if *he* does not raise them himself, *you* must.

Think up your own list of likely objections

The easiest way to observe the iceberg rule is to make your own list of likely objections and prepare answers to them accordingly. Then, if the buyer fails to raise these objections, you should raise them yourself and answer each of them, one by one.

When closing, offer the customer something specific to buy

Although this may sound a bit daft, many sales collapse only because the customer is not offered something specific to buy, or because he is given too many choices and becomes unable to make up his mind. Avoid this mistake by offering your customers something specific.

Examples

Henry owns a small business wholesaling garden tools to shops and garden centres. In the beginning, he used to supply his customers with whatever they wanted, in the quantities they wanted. He still does this with his established customers, but any new ones are offered a standard sales package that includes a basic assortment of the most popular tools. In effect, Henry asks new customers to say yes to a specific package.

Joy makes a range of handmade woollen pullovers and cardigans for sale to shops and larger department stores. Whenever she telephones a new customer, she offers him the choice of three standard packages, each containing a different number of woollen garments and priced accordingly.

Felix owns a dog kennels. He offers two standard services: a five-star luxury service or a very comfortable service – both available at daily or weekly rates. In addition, he offers a special Pampered Pet Weekend service, plus separate massage, grooming, and shampoo services. In short, Felix has something for any dog-owner to say yes to.

How to deal with abrupt or aggressive customers

In general, the more pleasant you are to people on the phone, the more pleasant they will be to you. However, if you use the phone a lot, sooner or later you are likely to encounter one or both of the following types of customer:

- The abrupt customer – who gives you the brush-off.
- The aggressive customer – who tells you to get lost.

The abrupt customer

The typical *Mr Abrupt* is almost certainly under some sort of pressure. He may be sitting in a crowded office; he may be in the middle of a meeting; he may be working hard to meet a deadline; he may be worried about his job, his wife, his car, or even his bladder; he may have just been disturbed by four different calls from four different salespeople; he may simply be feeling lazy. As a result, when you telephone, he usually makes no attempt to listen to what you have to say and simply says – 'Not interested!'

When you encounter Mr Abrupt, your best approach is as follows:

- Understand that your listener is under pressure.
- Try to convey your understanding down the phone and simply say something such as, 'Is this a bad time to call? I can easily ring back.'
- If your listener declines to suggest that you call back, try asking another question to find out the reason for his lack of interest. Provided you sound polite and friendly, you can usually get away with asking something such as, 'I'm sorry if I have caught you at a bad moment, but can I ask *why* you have no interest in my product?'

    At this point, the customer usually comes clean and tells you the problem. You may not be able to overcome it, but at least you will know how useful the customer is likely to be to you and you can react accordingly.
- The bottom line, when meeting Mr Abrupt, is this: always ask for the reason behind the abruptness and lack of interest. Never simply accept it at face value. If you do, you will lose sales.

    For example, a 'not interested, thank you ...' from the MD of a company may mean any or all of the following:

    - I'm on the other phone.
    - My secretary is away and the other phone is ringing.
    - Sales are massively down this month.
    - I've just lost a big customer – I can't think of anything else.
    - I've just won a huge new order – who cares about anything else.
    - The manager who normally deals with this is away.
    - I'm off to the races and I'm late already.

The aggressive customer

Mr Aggressive is not just uninterested in you and your product: he is positively antagonistic. He usually says something like – Oh no, not another bloody salesperson. Why don't you get lost and pester someone else?!

Now, poor old Mr Aggressive may be simply an extreme type of Mr Abrupt. Perhaps he has just been demoted or divorced or served with a winding-up order or given some abuse by another caller. Alternatively, he may simply be abrasive by nature. Whatever the reason for his intemperance, this is how you should handle him.

- As in the case of Mr Abrupt, try to defuse the situation by apologising for ringing at an obviously bad moment, and suggest that you call back at a more convenient time.
- If your listener agrees, try to get him to suggest a time for you. If, on the other hand, he continues to be aggressive, you should stand your ground and explain yourself as follows:
  - Tell him that he is no different from you. Both of you depend on new customers to stay in business. That means both of you are obliged to telephone new customers or else go bust and live off the state. And if he does not have to telephone new customers himself, he is bound to rely on other people to do it for him.
  - Tell him that you can appreciate that he may not be in the least bit interested in buying from you at the moment (despite the fact that he has no accurate idea of what you are selling and how he may benefit), but tell him that nearly all buyers need alternative suppliers, just in case. Remind him that the purpose of your call was not to sell him thousands of pounds worth of products (even if it was), but simply to introduce yourself and your product in order to give him the future option of buying from you.

If you can explain these two points to your opponent, you stand every chance of calming him down, gaining his respect and perhaps even making a sale. At the very least you will maintain your self-respect, which is just as important.

7

Sell more by learning the art of face-to-face selling

This is your sixth step to sales success. Learn the ultimate commercial art of selling yourself and your product to another human being, face to face.

The two most common types of face-to-face selling are: selling to a business customer in his office and selling to a private individual or couple in their home. This chapter covers both situations.

Face-to-face selling is the art of selling yourself

Human chemistry being what it is, when two people meet face to face anything can happen. Because of this, face-to-face selling will always be an art, not a science. This means, for example, that until you have a reasonable amount of experience in handling people, you may find some easy to sell to and others impossible. Do not worry about this in the slightest; it is only natural.

Despite our unpredictable chemistry, there are still a number of principles to observe when selling to someone in person. The first and most important of these, may be expressed thus:

- When selling to someone face to face, you sell yourself first.

    Or, to put it the other way round:

- Customers respond first to the salesperson, then to the product.

In other words, *you* and your personality are the conduit for your product. If *you* come across as friendly and professional, your buyer is likely to respond positively to both you and your product. By the same token, if you appear unfriendly or unprofessional, your buyer will have no hesitation in showing you the door, no matter how good your product may be.

One face-to-face business meeting is worth 100 telephone calls

There is no more effective way of making an impact on a business customer than to meet him and explain your product to him in person. There are two different reasons for this.

First, most buyers receive hundreds of phone calls from different salespeople every month. Because of this, most salespeople never succeed in making an individual impact on the buyer and remain simply a name on a piece of paper or a file in a filing cabinet.

By contrast, if you can win, for example, half an hour of the buyer's undivided attention then you (and your product) will mean something to him. Indeed, many buyers tend not to buy anything from salespeople whom they have not met personally. This is hardly surprising; after all, while a managing director may speak to 200 salespeople a month, over the phone, he is likely to meet fewer than 50. Now ask yourself which salespeople he is more likely to remember or which salespeople he is more likely to buy from?

Second, although the telephone is by far the cheapest and most effective method of canvassing and maintaining contact with customers, when it comes to more complex or problematic discussion, it cannot compare with a face-to-face meeting.

For example, you may sell a particular service whose effectiveness is heavily dependent on you and your knowledge. How are you going to do justice to your personal skill and expertise over the phone or on paper? Alternatively, if you are selling a new product, how can you convey its full potential down a phone line? Conversely, how can you properly appreciate the personal and commercial needs of a customer unless you see him (and/or his operation) in situ?

How to handle four typical buyers you are likely to meet

Although business buyers come in all different shapes and sizes, four common stereotypes are worth isolating for closer study. Although, obviously, you will also meet these four types over the phone as well as face to face, I have included their profiles in this chapter because their individual characteristics have a greater effect in person than down a telephone wire!

Mr By-the-Book

This sort of buyer (usually a senior manager) has a particularly high regard for his own status and the company procedures that support him.

Typically, he speaks to no one unless they have first sent him written details and given him sufficient time to digest them at his convenience. He has particularly firm views on what is worth buying and what is not, and rarely departs from them willingly. The good news about this buyer is that he takes pride in what he does and takes it seriously. Also, once you have established your bona fides as a supplier, you are likely to enjoy a long and uninterrupted business relationship with him and the company for whom he works.

How to handle Mr By-the-Book

- Show him the utmost respect at all times.
- Spoil him with personal but professional attention and service.
- Observe the corporate rigmarole and rules that he holds dear.
- Avoid giving your own opinion on any extraneous matters unless you feel certain that he will agree with you.
- Avoid making jokes unless you are certain he will laugh.
- Go out of your way to buttress his self-esteem.

Mr Familiar

This sort of buyer (usually a middle/senior manager) is often quite bored with his job and with what he buys. To him, the only consolation is meeting people who will laugh at his jokes, share a drink with him and generally uplift him. The good news about him is that he is far more approachable and suggestible than Mr By-the-Book and far better company. The bad news is that he is more changeable and may also be regarded with less respect by his bosses. In order to sustain a long-term business relationship with this sort of buyer, you are likely to have to pamper him continually with time and attention.

How to handle Mr Familiar

- Keep him interested and amused.

- Show interest in him and ask questions about his ambitions.
- Be firm and very positive about your product: he will respect you for it. A contrary opinion will never upset him.
- Spoil him with personal attention and occasional gifts for him and his wife.
- Be prepared to socialise/get drunk with him.

Mr Rational

This sort of buyer (anyone up to and including MD level) prides himself on his logical attitude to spending money. He would probably say that he buys the best products for the best price, irrespective of who is selling them. Thus, he tends to research and investigate what he buys and will often let would-be suppliers dangle for a time before coming to a decision in order to squeeze them for extra discount. Nevertheless, as a rational person, he is particularly attuned to the need to keep his own customers happy.

Thus, if you can present an excellent case for your product (and especially if you can demonstrate how it will help him to win more business), he will quite happily pay a proper price. The bad news about doing business with Mr Rational is that he is a continuously demanding customer. He will monitor your performance at every stage and allow you to get away with nothing. For example, if your invoices are inaccurate in any respect they will be returned for correction, at the last possible moment. It is, as he would say, the rational thing to do!

How to handle Mr Rational

- Exude professionalism at all times and from every pore.
- Be respectful but never obsequious.
- Prepare your presentation with the greatest of care; know your facts backwards. Role-play your answers to his inevitable objections. Above all, mug up on your competitors. In addition, never make promises that you are not certain of keeping.
- If any objections remain outstanding, make sure you return with a watertight answer.
- Never worry about offering a contrary opinion (on anything) to this buyer, provided you can back it up.

Mr Dynamic

This sort of buyer (anyone up to and including MD level) has immense faith in his own considerable abilities. Thus, if you can convince him of the effectiveness and reliability of what you are selling, he is inclined to make up his mind on the spot. In return, he expects an equally prompt reaction from others. Thus, you can expect him to ask you for an immediate quotation for a particular type of order, or to grill you on anything from your competitors' after-sales service to your own delivery dates.

Above all, this buyer does not suffer fools for more than a few moments. Your presentation must therefore be precise and to the point. Even then, he is almost certain to interrupt you at regular intervals. Although you should indulge him in this respect, you should also stand your ground where necessary. Like Mr Rational, Mr Dynamic admires people who stand up to him, provided they know their facts.

How to handle Mr Dynamic

- For a meeting with this buyer, always arrive early but expect the meeting to start late!
- As in the case of Mr Rational, be professional at all times.
- Have your wits sharpened and be ready with your facts and your calculator: you will need them all.
- Keep your presentation relevant; do not stray from the point.
- Stand your ground when pressurised, but if you are unsure of your facts or your answer – say so.
- With this buyer in particular, be sure to push for the order. If you give a good presentation, you may well get it.

Explanatory note

- These four mini-profiles are offered purely as a crude guide to the basic idiosyncrasies of the buyers in question and how to handle them. Thus, for example, where I stress the need to treat a particular buyer in a particularly professional manner, I do not thereby imply that other buyers may be treated *un*professionally. I simply wish to alert you to the former's exaggerated respect for the quality concerned.

- In this context, to behave in a 'professional' manner includes:
  - Arriving on time.
  - Having a well-groomed appearance.
  - Conducting yourself with courtesy and restraint.
  - Being familiar with the customer's market position and products.
  - Showing interest in the details of the customer's operation.
  - Being fingertip-ready with the facts of your product and those of your competitors.
  - Being able to defend and justify your arguments.
  - Showing a readiness to listen to contrary points.
  - Having the confidence to ask the customer to buy.

How to conduct a business sales meeting in the customer's office

Despite certain radical differences in the *way* you present yourself and your product to the customer, which we shall examine shortly, your *objectives* remain the same for a personal sales presentation as they are for a telephone presentation.

An outline of what to say

Imagine you own a six-car mini-cab company. You visit a local advertising and PR agency operating from a city centre office block.

- Relax your customer and get his attention by asking a few general questions about himself and his company.
- Once you feel that he is relaxed and that you have his attention, take control by telling him what you are going to do. For example, say something such as:
  - I'm going to explain what my firm can do for you and what services we provide, and then you will be able to decide how or to what extent it can help your business, all right? Now, first, could you tell me...?

    You now ask a number of prepared questions with the aim of finding out something about the customer's need for your service. Here is a small selection of questions you may ask, with the customer's replies in brackets.
  - How important is it to you to keep your customers happy and to provide them with a fast, comprehensive service? (Very.)
  - Does that mean you sometimes have to work to deadlines and have the job finished at a moment's notice? (Yes.)

- How often does this entail co-ordinating the movements of staff, customers, press people and so on? (Frequently.)
- Where are your main customers located? (In and around the city.)
- What method of transport do you and your staff currently use to get around the city during the day? (Company cars.)
- How easy do you find parking? (Generally OK, but sometimes it is difficult.)
- How often does that entail your staff leaving early to arrive for meetings on time? (Sometimes.)
- How often do you organise lunchtime presentations or evening functions? (Quite frequently.)
- How often is alcohol served at these occasions? (Frequently.)
- How often do your staff/your customers leave these functions over the alcohol limit? (No comment!)
- Possibly quite often? (Possibly.)
- How do they usually get back home or to their offices? (By taxi.)
- Do you currently have a standing arrangement with another mini-cab/taxi firm to transport your staff/your customers, if needed? (No.)
- So presumably you call for a taxi when required and pay the standard rate? (Yes.)
- And if, perhaps because of bad weather, there are no taxis available, you and your customers may have to wait? (Yes.)

You may continue to probe for additional needs, for example, how often the customer needs to despatch urgent artwork materials (that cannot be transported by motorbike), or how often he needs to transport visiting clients to and from hotels, etc.

- Summarise and repeat back to the customer those points that you think are important to him: ie, his needs. For example, in the light of the above you may say:

- If I understand you correctly, because of the nature of your business, one of your main priorities is to be able to react swiftly and effectively to the needs of your clients, is that right? I mean, the faster and better your reaction, the more business you are likely to get, is that right? (The customer really has to say yes to both these questions.)

- OK, here's what we can do to improve the service you offer your clients ....
- You now list the most important features of your mini-cab service, taking care to relate them to the customer's overall need to react swiftly and effectively to the demands of his clients, and using the information you have obtained about the details of his current operation.

  For example, your general approach may be as follows:
- First, deal with lunchtime and evening functions. Explain how you can collect/drop off his customers and staff, thus avoiding any breathalyser problems, saving customer and staff time and saving money on standard taxi fares.
- Second, deal with situations involving rush-jobs. Paint a picture of a situation when the colour design of a particular advertisement is rejected by a client at the last minute, and new copy has to be prepared, sent back to the client for approval and then sent on to the printers.

  Obviously, the agency has arrangements in hand for such situations but emphasise the desirability of having a mini-cab company in support for emergencies. Also, point out that it may be a lot cheaper to have a cab driver ferry artwork materials from A to B and back to A, than to have a member of staff do it.
- Third, impress upon the customer how having a cab company on contract can help him to increase the number of services he offers to clients. Paint a picture of, for example, a local race meeting at which he wants to entertain various clients. Instead of having his senior account handlers drive all over the city, rounding up clients and taking them to the meeting, he just needs to make one phone call to your cab company and bingo: the clients are picked up and driven straight to the agency's hospitality area on the course. Meanwhile, his senior staff can continue with other productive tasks.
- Fourth, show the customers a few testimonials from some of your other satisfied customers, praising the efficiency of your cab service and testifying to how it has helped them save valuable time and money.
- Finally, you may end your presentation by saying that even though these are only some of the benefits you can offer the customer (allude to future plans) you expect that he has a

number of queries or questions about your service which you will do your best to answer.

- You now listen carefully to any objections and deal with them, using the Welcome-Probe-Test-Answer method. If, by any chance, the customer chooses not to raise any objections and you feel that his restraint is not genuine, raise one or two yourself and then answer them.
- Finally, whether or not you believe that the customer is 100 per cent convinced, you must push for the order and close the sale.
- In the event that the customer side-steps your attempts to close by saying, 'I'll have to think about it', you should *always* probe to find out whether this reply means, Yes, No, Maybe or Don't know. Never accept it simply on face value.

  For example, ask something like:
  - How do you feel about what I've told you?
  - Does everything sound OK, or is there something you're not quite sure about?
  - Is there anything you're not 100 per cent sure about?

The dos and don'ts of selling face to face to a business customer

Dress neutrally and ensure you are well groomed

Whatever you choose to wear, make sure it is not likely to distract the customer and thus deflect attention from what you are saying. For example, avoid garish ties, greasy shirt collars, power-jewellery, short skirts and dirty shoes.

The same goes for your grooming. For example, noticeable hair styles are out, so are Zapata moustaches and Fu Manchu beards. In short, be noticed for your sales presentation not for your appearance.

Arrive early and use your waiting time constructively

Never arrive just on time for a meeting. By the time the receptionist has found your host and announced you, you will already be late!

Instead, try to arrive at least five to ten minutes early, make any final adjustments to yourself before leaving your car and then keep your eyes open while you wait in reception. For example, flick through any customer magazines or brochures lying around. If you can acquire any bang-up-to-date information on the customer, you will almost certainly be able to use it in your meeting and impress the customer accordingly. In the absence of any company magazines, look out for any awards or photographs on the walls.

Lastly, while waiting in reception, I recommend that you stay standing and avoid the temptation to sink (slump) into the nearest sofa. Rising clumsily to greet your customer is unlikely to create the best of first impressions.

Shaking hands and establishing eye contact with the customer

Always observe this ritual and, if necessary, take the initiative. When shaking hands, try not to use either the bone-crusher or the dead-fish grip. Incidentally, from this moment onward you are definitely on-camera. From hereon, therefore, you must establish and maintain eye contact with the customer.

Take the initiative on the way to the customer's office

Sometimes, on the way to the customer's office, you will get the opportunity to see a part of his company in action. Seize this with both hands! Ask whether the customer would be kind enough to give you a mini-tour. By doing this, not only are you likely to learn a great deal about the customer's operation, but also in turn your interest is likely to be noticed and appreciated by him.

Start the meeting on a friendly note and involve the customer

Nearly all customers instinctively respond well to a friendly salesperson. So smile and do your best to start the meeting on a friendly note.

At the same time, involve the customer by immediately asking a few general questions about himself and his company. Recent research shows that questions containing the word *you* are far more likely to arouse interest in the listener than questions containing the word *I*.

Avoid sending the wrong body signals to your customer

According to experts, body language accounts for an astonishing 70 per cent of the impact of your message on your listener. Even if they are only half right, you are going to communicate a huge amount without uttering a word, so pay attention to the following tips.

How to communicate openness and honesty

Most body linguists say that openness and honesty are nearly always conveyed by someone with palms held open or, at the very least, with hands openly on view. Conversely, speakers who hide their hands convey secrecy or deceit.

In general, the more closed or defensive your body position, the more defensive your attitude. Thus, arms folded across your chest or a hand held in front of your face are interpreted as defensive gestures conveying a lack of openness.

The moral? If you want to impress your customer with your honesty, leave your chest and face open and undefended, and keep your hands visible at all times.

How to communicate confidence

If the idea of thumping your chest and giving out a few Tarzan-like howls does not appeal to you, try a less energetic gesture. Place your elbows on the table and make a steeple with your hands. Experts state that this gesture represents an unequivocal statement of confidence.

How to show interest

This is done in several small ways. First, and most important, always maintain eye contact with the person talking. Second, lean slightly forward. Third, tilt your head slightly to one side. Lastly, do not fidget.

Use sales aids to reinforce your message

A sales aid can be anything from an official video of your company to a typed piece of paper containing a list of benefits that the customer will receive from buying your product. It can also be a written testimonial from one of your satisfied customers; it can also be a sample of your product.

The importance of sales aids lies in their visual impact on the customer opposite. Remember, we forget up to 80 per cent of what we hear (as opposed to what we see), within 24 hours.

The moral? Think creatively about what sales aids you can design to help explain your business and put across your message.

Warning: keep control over your sales aids

For example, never simply hand your sales brochure to a customer unless you are prepared for him to spend the next few minutes glancing through it, oblivious to your accompanying commentary.

Similarly, if you pull out a copy of your sales brochure together with a pencil to direct the customer's attention to a particular sentence or paragraph (a good idea), do not wave the pencil about or leave the brochure on view while you talk. They will quickly become distractions in the eyes of your listener.

Watch out for danger signs while speaking

Lack of attention

Research shows that when a listener crosses his arms, his attention to what is being said falls by between 35 and 40 per cent. As a result, his attitude becomes increasingly negative. Your best approach, when you see your listener adopting this position, is to offer him something to hold or look at and thus compel him to uncross his arms.

Disinterest/disbelief

This is typically conveyed by a number of different gestures. These include: turning slightly away from the speaker, leaning backwards, keeping the head down and crossing the chest in a defensive manner. The more of these that your listener adopts, the greater his disinterest or disbelief. Once again, your best reaction is to involve the listener in some way (for example, ask him one or two questions or hand him something to force him to change position).

The dos and don'ts of selling face to face in the home

This section covers the most common form of face-to-face selling in the home, namely: the sale of personal services by self-employed craftsmen such as plumbers, painters and decorators, electricians, small builders and so on.

Why every craftsman should learn how to sell

Having the skill to install a central-heating system is one thing; having the skill to sell it to a customer is quite another. Unfortunately, the latter skill is paramount. I say 'unfortunately' because, while many craftsmen are experts in their particular craft, very few (in my experience) are organised enough to communicate this expertise to their customers.

For instance, imagine yourself in the position of the customer:

- Due to a lack of maintenance, one of the pipes in your central heating springs a leak. It is 2pm. You panic and reach for your *Yellow Pages*. You dial the numbers of five plumbers – in vain. Either there is no reply or someone answers and says, 'The-plumber-is-out-can-he-call-you-back-when-he-returns?' You leave a message and pace the floor in your wellingtons.
- By 5pm you can wait no longer. You redial the five numbers plus a couple more for good measure. Still no sign of a plumber. Your frustration is compounded when one of the plumbers' wives explains that there is really no point in ringing before at least 7pm.
- Finally, at 7pm, one of the plumbers (Fred) telephones and arranges to come round within the hour.
- At 8.15pm, Fred arrives, makes various disparaging noises about the unserviced state of the central-heating system, repairs the leak, gives you a hefty 'minimum call-out' bill, takes the money and goes home for a (presumably) well-earned rest.
- You are left to stew over a large bill and the fact that your heating system needs a service. You are unlikely to be left feeling good about plumbers!

Points to note

- Pipes burst around the clock and sometimes need urgent attention. *If you are a plumber* and you want the business (which according to your *Yellow Pages* advertisement you do), you must organise yourself so as to be able to react in time. In the above example, Fred simply happened to be the first to call. In fact, Tom, Dick and Harry – three other plumbers – rang after Fred, only to find that the job had already gone.

- When receiving a customer enquiry, remember: you are in a *selling* situation, so *sell yourself!*
- When following up a customer enquiry on the phone, remember: you are in a *selling* situation, so *sell yourself!*
- When entering (the privacy of) the customer's home, remember: you are in a *selling* situation, so *sell yourself!*
- When saying goodbye to a customer, remember: you are *still* in a *selling* situation, so *sell yourself!*

What Fred should do

- When either he or his wife or his assistant answers the phone at 2pm, they should react professionally as follows:
  - They should ask for precise details of the problem, plus the customer's exact address/telephone number/name.
  - They should reassure the customer that Fred will sort it out, then list the steps that the customer should take to stop the problem getting any worse.
  - They should say that Fred will call no later than, say, 8pm, but will try to get there sooner.
- Ideally, although this may not always be feasible, the person should ring later to reassure the customer that Fred will definitely be over by 8pm. Apart from making the customer feel spoilt for service (despite the fact that no plumber has yet arrived), this call also enables you to double-check that no other plumber is/will be called out by the customer.
- Upon returning from his day work, Fred should phone the customer, thank him for his enquiry and explain that he is on his way over.
- When he finally arrives, Fred should take a moment to sell himself by complimenting the customer on his home and sympathising with his burst-pipe problem.
- After completing the repair, Fred should then explain – for the customer's future reference – what the problem was, how it happened and what the customer can do (if anything) to prevent a recurrence. Regarding the unserviced state of the heating system as a whole, he should explain to the customer exactly what needs doing, why, and roughly how much it will cost. He should then suggest that he returns to service it on such and such a day.
- When presenting the customer with the bill, Fred should make the

point that he will lower his charges a little for any future business
and reassure the customer that, if the heating system is serviced
properly and regularly, he is unlikely to incur such bills in the
future.

- When taking his leave, Fred should thank the customer for his
business and say that unless pipes burst occasionally he would not
have a plumbing business. Finally, he should hand the customer a
business card/leaflet with details of how to contact him in the
future.

The lesson? If you are a craftsman, you must sell, sell, sell!

From a sales viewpoint, a homeowner with a burst pipe is in the same
position as a person who walks into a car showroom. Both are looking to buy and both must be sold to. So, if you are a craftsman, do as
the car salesman does and get used to the idea of selling your service
properly and professionally. Thus, if a customer phones with an
enquiry of some kind, try this:

- Start thinking about the customer. Many customers know very
little about how to fix burst pipes (or, for that matter, electrical
malfunctions or leaking roofs or cracks in walls or crumbling plas-
ter, etc). They simply see a messy problem that threatens to get
worse.

  What most of them need, first and foremost, is reassurance:
reassurance that their problem is solvable and that you will solve
it as quickly as possible. So when a customer rings, make sure that
he receives reassurance. Give a customer peace of mind (even if
he has to wait a few hours) and in return he is likely to repay you,
many times over, with his future business.
- Get the details of the customer and the job and write them down.
- Respect the privacy of the customer's home. Many customers
instinctively feel awkward about inviting strangers into their
homes. So when arriving, use your common sense and try to relax
them and dispel their awkwardness by making a few nice comments about their house.
- Involve the customer. Ask him one or two questions about himself
(for example, How long have you been in this house?), then ask
about the job itself. You may already know something about it,

but ask for as much information as you can. If the customer wants you to quote for something, you must try to find out exactly what he wants. If you can do this, you stand an excellent chance of having your quote accepted.

A good method of flushing out this information is to involve the customer by explaining that the job can be done in three different ways: very thoroughly, quite thoroughly or cheaply. Ask him which approach he wants you to take. In addition, ask him when he would like the job done.

- Try to close the sale on your first visit. Many craftsmen make the mistake of leaving the customer, once they know the details of the job, and phoning through a quotation the following day. This may be unavoidable, but if at all possible you should give the customer an approximate quote on the spot and try to get him to accept it, *there and then*.

Although most customers appreciate the value of getting several quotes for a particular job, many will quite happily accept one quote from *someone they feel comfortable with*. Now you can understand why you have gone to such prior trouble to reassure and relax the customer. You want to make the customer feel comfortable with you.

Conclusion

The fundamental principle of successful selling

Nearly all the ideas and advice contained in this book are based upon the following fundamental principle:

Selling is all about communicating with customers; thus, in order to sell more, you must improve the way in which *you and your business* communicate with your customers.

Take action today!

Why not put this principle into practice today? Try this exercise: ask yourself the following eight questions:

1. Do I have the telephone numbers of *all* my customers?
2. Do they *all* have details of *all* my products/services?
3. Am I making it *easy* for them to contact me?
4. Do I know *exactly* what to say when a customer calls?
5. Do I have something *in writing* about my company to show to a customer?
6. Do I always try to interest my present customers in *my full range* of products/services?
7. Do I *maintain regular contact* with *all* my present customers?
8. Do I *regularly* make a point of trying to contact new customers before they contact me?

If you answer 'No' to any of these questions, you have immediately highlighted a weakness in the way in which you communicate with your customers. By remedying this weakness, you will almost certainly see your sales improve.

Start today, and you will never look back!

Further Reading from Kogan Page

Auer, J T: *Inspired Selling: A Book of Ideas, Opportunities and Renewal*

Denny, Richard: *Selling to Win: Tested Techniques for Closing the Sale*

Golis, Christopher C: *Empathy Selling: The Powerful New Technique for the 1990s*

Hopkins, Leon: *Budgeting for Business*
                       Cash Flow And How To Improve It

Johnson, Neil: *The Secrets of Telephone Selling*

Ley D Forbes: *The Best Seller*

Sadgrove, Kit: *Seductive Selling*

Schiffman, Stephan: *The 25 Most Common Sales Mistakes ... and How to Avoid Them*

Thomson, Peter: *Sell Your Way to the Top*

Tirbutt, Edmund: *How to Increase Sales Without Leaving Your Desk*

Vicar, Robert: *First Division Selling*
                  Prospecting for Customers

Weymes, Pat: *How to Perfect Your Selling Skills*

A full list is available from the publisher.

Index